THE NAKED TRUTH: JESUS'S KINGDOM OF GOD AND ITS MYSTERIES DECODED

The New Gospel Revelations Series 1

The New Gospel Revelations Series *of* the *New* Christianity of Christ *Essentials* Made Easy
The Words and Works of Jesus Christ Decoded

Festus Enumah M.D.

The New Gospel Revelations Series of the New Christianity of
Christ *Essentials* Made Easy
The Words and Works of Jesus Christ Decoded
The Naked *Truth:* Jesus's Kingdom of God and its Mysteries Decoded
The New Gospel Revelations Series 1
Copyright © 2016
Authored by Festus Enumah M.D.
All rights reserved.
ISBN: 069275220X
ISBN 13: 9780692752203

For information regarding permission, write to:
Festus Enumah, M.D.
1629 10th Avenue. Columbus. GA 31901. USA

Library of Congress Control Number: 2016914281
Festus Enumah, Columbus, GA

DEDICATION

This book is dedicated to:
Jesus Christ, His twelve apostles and Paul whose
works I have reported in this book

Other books by Festus Enumah M.D.

The Innocent Blood and Judas Iscariot
The Father's Business and the Spiritual Cross

Coming soon.
Complete Volume (The New *Gospel* Revelations Series 1-5) of the New Christianity of Christ Essentials-Made Easy
The Words and Works of Jesus Christ Decoded
The New *Gospel* Revelations Series 2 –Easter Decoded: Jesus's Everlasting Miracle of the Earthly Stages of Human Creation
The New *Gospel* Revelations Series 3-*ABC's of Eternal Life. **Jesus's Role in Human Creation
The New *Gospel* Revelations Series 4-The Mysteries of Golgotha: Why Jesus Died
The New Revelations Series 5-An Exemplary Christian: *the German Chancellor Angela
Merkel. **What makes you *NOT* a Christian.

ABOUT THE BOOK COVER

Front Cover

The spiritual events in Jerusalem and at Golgotha carried all the divine portraits of the Father's business and placed them conspicuously in the human consciousness for everlasting remembrance. Jesus performed many healing miracles with the power of His Kingdom of God. It is for these reasons that the book cover was designed, bearing with it, the Oath of Hippocrates, shaped in the form of a cross.

The image is from a 12ᵗʰ century Byzantine manuscript. Vatican Bibloteca Apostolica, Rome.

Back Cover

The back cover of the book portrays the footprints of the twelve ordained apostles, whose feet Jesus washed during the Last Supper in preparation for their travel to the Greco-Roman Empire and to all parts of the world, in order to spread the good news of Jesus's Kingdom of God.

CONTENTS

INTRODUCTION

The Kingdom of God that Jesus proclaimed two thousand years ago in Palestine was a historic and unprecedented event. Its introduction marked the moment in the history of mankind, when for the first time, the human souls, bound in darkness and caged in ignorance about the spiritual worlds, saw light. Those who recognized the meaning of it and received it, leaped, rejoiced and manifested its power. When Jesus demonstrated the power of that Kingdom, the people were amazed and asked: "what thing is this? What new doctrine is this? For with authority He commanded even the unclean spirits, and they do obey Him." (Mark 1:27)

People never heard of the new Kingdom of God. What Jesus introduced was completely new. Jesus portrayed and preached this Kingdom in parables, metaphors and in symbolic expressions. All the parables of the Kingdom of God carry infinite messages for mankind. As you explore them, you cannot but wonder what is beyond those words of wisdom. With power and authority, unmatched in the history of mankind, Jesus successfully demonstrated the meaning of that Kingdom of God. However, the ubiquitous *modus operandi* used by Jesus to reveal the meaning of the new Kingdom of God confused many people. It is for this reason, coupled with our inability to interpret the parables and metaphors associated with it, that no one has given satisfactory interpretation to the meaning of Jesus's Kingdom of God. Many books have been written and many sermons preached on Jesus's Kingdom of God. They all have been given many different interpretations.

I have written this book to reveal what I recovered from the Gospel as the true meaning of the Kingdom of God that Jesus proclaimed and to show why the true knowledge on that Kingdom of God is vital. It was so important that the Father sent Jesus to proclaim it, demonstrate it, prescribe how we can get it and reveal its intrinsic infinite importance in human life. Jesus suffered and died that we may have that vital information and participates in it. Jesus's Kingdom of God is in everything. The Spirit of the Father is in it. The Spirit of Jesus Christ is in it. The human spirit is in it. You are in it. All human beings are in it. A human soul without it is dead. This is the knowledge we must use to advance our intelligence as to stop killing one another, seek peace instead of war to settle conflicts, deploy compassion and love as weapons for global sufferings that manifest in many forms. Human knowledge and experience of Jesus's Kingdom of God, instantaneously provides the platform for all Christians and their leaders to demonstrate to the world by the epitome of their lives, what Jesus prescribed, proclaimed and revealed. The glorious future that awaits all mankind depends on it.

What is revealed in Jesus's Kingdom of God enables one to have a glimpse into the mysteries of the death and the resurrection of Jesus. It provided a platform on which one can stand to know who Jesus is and the Father that He revealed to the world. It enables the reader not only to have knowledge of who we are, why we are here, but also to look beyond the present visible world and perceive the bond that binds all human souls together with the Spirit of the Father and Jesus Christ. Paul used the lens of this Kingdom to look into the future and proclaimed that he was persuaded that, "neither death, nor life, nor angels, nor principalities, nor powers, nor things present, nor things to come, nor height. Nor depth, nor any other creation, shall be able to separate us from the love of God, which is in Christ Jesus our Lord." (Romans 8:38-38) After his experience with the risen Christ on his way to Damascus, Paul live completely under the shadow of Jesus's Kingdom of God and manifested by his life examples, all its features as prescribed, proclaimed and demonstrated by Christ.

Jesus's Kingdom of God is the way through which all generations-regardless of nationality, ethnicity and religious background-will develop and advance our intelligence that would really benefit mankind. This would enable us in this 21st century, to stop all our evil activities against one another and recognize the equality of all mankind bound together by the Spirit of the new God-the Father-that Jesus revealed to the world. The advances in science and technology have done nothing for human being but have lead to the production of weapons of mass destruction, fear for our lives, divisions among nations, wars, increase in the population of refugees, extreme greed and increase in the population of families that live on less than one dollar a day. The suicide rate is sky rocketing in many developed nations. A new phone, a million dollar home, a private jet, billions of dollars in private accounts, money laundering have no intrinsic value to human life. Advances of our intelligence based on the features in Jesus's Kingdom of God, enhance the intrinsic value of human life and in future will leads to the quest-as suggested by Christ-to be as perfect as the Father.

What Jesus accomplished by His death and resurrection would not be possible without the power of the Kingdom of God that He proclaimed. That Kingdom of God is the power behind all Jesus's words and works. Without it we are nothing. With it we are guaranteed to have life and have it abundantly. The lack of knowledge of Jesus's Kingdom of God and its mysteries posed a great obstacle to what Jesus prescribed, demonstrated and revealed. It has caused division instead of unity among the Christians and their leaders. It promulgated and encouraged the introduction of human doctrines and dogmas into the divine doctrines of Christ. The lack of knowledge of the vital information led to the misinterpretations of the death of Jesus and incomplete interpretation of His resurrection. I have written this book to share this vital information with the reader. Many people in the time of Jesus believed that He proclaimed a real Kingdom of God that was to come in this world where His Father was to reign. Today, many Christians are still waiting for the second coming of Christ to establish that Kingdom. Perhaps, if the real meaning of Jesus's Kingdom of God was handed down to us, the evils of the last two thousand years would not have occurred.

You can help.

It is my hope that you would disseminate the information to others. This is the time to make disciples of all nations with this vital information that will help everyone in the journey to God, the Father of Jesus Christ. It is the information that will help us avert errors and inappropriate attitudes towards one another, promoting love and peace instead of war and hatred.

CHAPTER 1

JESUS CHRIST AND HIS KINGDOM OF GOD

The entire preaching of Jesus before His death and after His death and resurrection concentrated on His Kingdom of God. A. M. Hunter, in his book on the *Work and Words of Jesus* commented on Jesus's teaching on the Kingdom of God:

> *One phrase sums up the meaning of our Lord's mission and message: His Kingdom of God. If we can discover what Jesus meant by it, we have the key to the Gospels and indeed to the whole New Testament.*

> ---A. M. Hunter

> *The crisis of Christian identity asks for a radical inquiry into the origin of its history. We need a fresh look at the main topic of Jesus's proclamation and ministry, the Kingdom of God. Any theological treatise (e.g., church, Christ, sacraments) has to be treated and developed from this center of Jesus' preaching, lest we get lost in all kinds of needless explanations and useless speculations."*

> ---John Fuellenbach. P. 5 the book: *Kingdom of God*

`There are many varied interpretations of Jesus's Kingdom of God in literature. I chose not to discuss all the current concepts of the Kingdom of God for this simple reason: exposition of it would be a hindrance in revealing to the readers, what I recovered from the Gospel on the Kingdom of God. The basic impulse behind the messages and the works of Christ centered on the Kingdom of God. It does not denote an area in the visible or invisible Universe where the God who rules the Universe resides, and from where He reigns. God has been ruling since the beginning of time. The Kingdom of God proclaimed by Jesus is not the rule of God. The introduction of Jesus's Kingdom of God marked a turning point in the history of humankind when holy armament for God-human creative Spiritual force from the Father, was placed at our disposal by Jesus Christ. It was the defining moment in history when God's design-the human creative architectural design-for all humanity was unfolded. The history of humanity is essentially the history of persistent and continuous God-human creation and experience. It is irrepressible and under the directorship of the Father and Jesus Christ.

The starting point for the ultimate understanding and interpretation of Jesus's Kingdom of God is to find out what He did for mankind with our gift from His Father: the Spirit of His Father in Him. Jesus's Kingdom of God is the life of His mission. Its objectives must be applicable to everything that Jesus did, including His death and resurrection. After Jesus's ascension, all efforts on Jesus Christ and His works, concentrated on His person, His death and resurrection. Christianity of Faith and Hope evolved. Without any meaningful understanding of Jesus's Kingdom of God, all those efforts put us in the position that we are today: lack of knowledge of what Jesus prescribed, proclaimed and demonstrated. The solution to gain knowledge of Jesus's words and works as I will reveal in this epistemology of this treatise is to look at both the cross and Jesus's Kingdom of God. Behind that cross is the power of that Kingdom of God.

The story of Jesus's Kingdom of God, is the story of the journey of the human soul to His Father. If you want to participate in that journey, you must first manifest that kingdom of God. Albert Schweitzer quoted by John Fullenbach in his book, *the Kingdom of God*, stated it in this way "As for humankind today, the realization of the Kingdom of God on earth has become a matter of survival or extinction."

Jesus's Kingdom of God reveals what Jesus did with the gift His Father gave Him for us. Jesus metaphorically used the word 'fire' to describe that gift. "I came to bring fire on the earth, and what will I if it is already kindled." (Luke 12:49) Jesus's Kingdom of God is the key to the whole Christian faith. Without it, any interpretation of the Christian faith becomes useless speculations. Christianity as prescribed, proclaimed and demonstrated by Christ, offers to the people of the world, something that other religions do not have. That element is Jesus's kingdom of God. It is the only Spiritual force, whose objective is to unite all worlds' communities, regardless of religious, tribal, or cultural differences. Without Jesus's Kingdom of God, human life as you know it today would not exist. It is the tool that mankind can use to fight worldwide human right abuses. The only thing that would break that evil thread is full knowledge and the experience of Jesus's Kingdom of God. It is only then that mankind would realize that to kill or abuse another human being is to destroy what the Father and Jesus Christ are creating; and to love that merciful Father of Jesus, is to love all people, even the enemy. It gives us the courage to live, knowing we are not alone in this world.

The Kingdom of God is the special spiritual tool that Jesus used to complete the Father's business of creation using Himself as an example. It was spiritual from its source, spiritual in what it was used for and spiritual in what it produced. It was the platform on which the Temple of the Father was erected without human hands. Embedded in it are imprints of the Spirit that Jesus brought down from the Father. Many of the features of the imprints are still hidden and will be revealed to future generations according to the will of the Father, when the time is fulfilled. With the introduction of the Kingdom of God came the light: the *magnum lux fiat*. There was indeed a great Light! Jesus's fascination with His Kingdom of God is unparalleled. To Jesus, it is life in itself. "If I by the finger of God cast out devils, no doubt the Kingdom of God is come upon you." (Luke 11:20) He associated His very personality with it.

Jesus's Kingdom of God is the paradise of the human soul in which one finds the meaning and purpose of human life. It is the platform on which one must stand to find the truth on how the Father and Jesus Christ are creating us; and having found it, to rejoice with friends and neighbors, and proclaim it to the world. In seeking the truth and the righteousness of this Kingdom, the Father and Jesus Christ are revealed and His love and glory are made manifest. The introduction of the Gospel of the Kingdom by Jesus of Nazareth marked the epoch when God fulfilled His promise to fully create us, through Jesus Christ, in spiritual human form, the spiritual imagery of Himself.

Jesus's Kingdom of God divine directive is the most important commandments ever given to humans that reveal the way to eternal life. It came down from heaven in the form of iridescent, heavenly light and shines into the transcendent human souls. It is like rain and snow that came down from heaven and then returned to God after their five thousand miles fruitful journey, bearing a basket that ascended to God holding the fully created spirits of His children, who received the blessing of His Spirit through Jesus Christ, by the obedience to His will.

Jesus's Kingdom of God is the spiritual gift from the Father that pushes all things to perfection. This perfection is, as the Father planned: the creation of spiritual human beings. It creates the whirlwind that moves the Father-human fellowship toward its heavenly abode. Whoever is given this Kingdom, will be called the merciful, the pure in heart, the peacemaker, and the children of God. They will in future, be joint heirs with the angels in Paradise. "He that keeps my commandment it is he that loves me, and he that loves me shall be loved by my Father, and I will love him and will manifest myself to him, if a man loves me, he will keep my words (the words that are spirit and of life) and my Father will love him and we will come unto him, and make our abode with him." (John 14: 21–23

The mission of Jesus started with the proclamation of "the Kingdom of God" and with the zeal to preach the Gospel of the Kingdom of God in all cities and villages in Palestine. As Jesus worked to get the message out, He said to the Apostles: "Let us go into the next towns that I may preach there also; for therefore came I forth." (Mark 1:38) The message was delivered in synagogues, on the streets, in the fields, by the seaside, on weekends and on Sabbath days. Even after His resurrection, Jesus continued to preach of things pertaining to the Kingdom of God. His final instruction to His selected apostles was "to go into the entire world and preach the gospel (of this kingdom) to every creature." (Mark 16:15) The Kingdom of God was very important to Jesus. Jesus insisted, again and again, that the Kingdom of God is a priori to our authentic life, and that we must live with it, move with it, both now and in the future. In short the essence of our being is the Kingdom of God.

As I searched the Gospel literature, it became obvious that there was no passage that revealed that at one time Jesus called the people together and discussed in plain Hebrew or Aramaic language the true meaning of the Kingdom of God. What the Gospel revealed is that the Kingdom of God as emphasized by Jesus is like something that cannot be destroyed, an entity designed in mosaic pattern, with the parables and comparative expressions as supportive frame work. Why couldn't Jesus have spoken plainly or call the people together and reveal what truly is the Kingdom of God.

Jesus turned to parables, metaphors, figurative expressions and miracles to convey what He could not say overtly on the meaning of the Kingdom of God as to protect Himself and what He came to accomplish. Unfortunately, detailed exposition of the parables of the Kingdom offered no assistance in the revelation of what Jesus's Kingdom of God is. I fell into that trap. I read all the parable narratives in the Gospel, and reviewed many texts from books on the Parables of Jesus. This I can tell you now, without going into details at this time, that when the truth of what the Kingdom is, that I recovered from the words and deeds of Christ, is applied to all His parables of the Kingdom, the entire parables-not one, but all-sparkle like the Polar stars that guide you in the journey of your soul to its glorious end. That was Jesus's purpose in using the parables to illuminate and empower the human souls to seek the Kingdom of God that came.

The Gospel of this Kingdom is one of the touchstones of Jesus' message but delivered to us in a six dimensional puzzle pattern. It is the forgotten foundation of the Christian piety. Perhaps, if Jesus had revealed to His audience, the true meaning of the terminology 'the Kingdom of God', it would be a bombshell that would send Jesus to the bottom floor of the Dead Sea and destroy His mission.

Unto what is the Kingdom of God like, and where unto shall I resemble it? It is like a grain of mustard seed, which a man took, and cast into his garden; and it grew and waxed a great tree; and the fowls of the air lodged in the branches of it,

---Luke 13 :18- 19.

Jesus understood His people very well. By His policy of silence on the meaning of the kingdom of God, Jesus denied the Jewish authority to trample and stampede in the garden where the mustard seed was planted. Obedience to His Father's command was the trademark of Jesus's spiritual professionalism. He would not reveal to the public the meaning of the kingdom of God but spoke of it and manifested the power if it as His Father directed. "For I have not spoken of myself; but the Father which sent me, he gave me a commandment, what I should say, and what I should speak." (John 12:49) The truth, my dear reader, is that if Jesus had lived for two thousand years and continued to preach on the kingdom of God, it would be impossible for us to comprehend it. Jesus demonstrated the power of that Kingdom by miracles. If Jesus's words on the Kingdom of God and His demonstration of its power are the elements needed for us to understand the meaning of it, then the meaning of it would be known today. Jesus revealed the meaning of the Kingdom of God to the apostles. As Christianity evolves, the meaning of Jesus's kingdom of God and its mysteries was lost. For many years after the crucible period of Christianity, we have searched in wrong places.

Jesus' Gospel of the Kingdom is like a candle that was lit and set upon the hilltop of a city. It gives light, both to the Jews and the Gentiles, to the small and the great, the poor and the rich, the just and the unjust, the colonizers and those colonized and to people irrespective of their creed, race and nationality. This light guides you to the intrinsic God-human spiritual bondage. This bondage prepares the humans for presentation to the Father in our next spiritual realm. But first, you must behave like the apostles, and develop spiritual eyes and spiritual ears as to be able to perceive this light and feel its vibrations. "Follow me, I am the light of the world," Jesus. We must follow Jesus, not only to find the meaning of the Kingdom of God but why His Father sent Him to us. We must follow him to find who Jesus is and have knowledge of the new God that He called His Father.

Know you not that ye are the temple of God, and that the Spirit of God dwells in you?

---1 Corinthian 3:16

And seek not ye what ye shall eat, or what ye shall drink, neither be ye of doubtful mind. For all these things do the nations of the world seek after: and your Father knoweth that ye have need of these things. But rather seek ye the kingdom of God; and all these things shall be added unto you.

---Luke 12: 29-31

Who is Jesus Christ?

We need a little knowledge on Jesus Christ, as to comprehend what His Kingdom of God is. Jesus, like His Father remained hidden from mankind until two thousand years ago when He made His appearance in Palestine. He told the Jews that, "Ye neither know me, nor my Father: if ye had known me, ye should have known my Father also. (John 8:19) The Prophet Esaias did not see any glory of Christ as was reported: "But though he had done so many miracles before them, yet they believed not on him: That the saying of Esaias the prophet might be fulfilled, which he spoke, Lord, who hath believed our report? And to whom hath the arm of the Lord been revealed? These things said Esaias, when he saw his glory, and spoke of him." (John 12:37, 38, 41) The report that Jesus was revealed by Moses and the Prophets and information about Him written in laws of Moses and in the Psalms is not true as was reported in the encounter between Jesus and the Jews; "these are the words which I spoke unto you, while I was yet with you, that all things must be fulfilled, which were written in the law of

Moses, and in the prophets, and in the psalms, concerning me." (Luke 24:44) If the reports are true, the Jews would not have condemned Jesus to death. All those reports are interpolations in an attempt to link Jesus to the God that Moses and the Prophets of Israel revealed.

The Jews do not believe that Jesus is the expected Jewish Messiah or the 'Anointed One of Israel.' If the Jews believed in the revealed glory of Christ or in any of the above titles for Jesus, they would not have condemned Him to death. What baffles me is this: the Christians do not know much about the Jewish religion, yet they embraced and used the Old Testament texts as framework in the interpretations of the words and works of Jesus.

Though I bear record of myself, yet my record is true: for I know whence I came, and whither I go; but ye cannot tell whence I come, and whither I go.

---John 8:14

The truth is that the Jews never heard of the Father or Jesus Christ before Jesus came, I will show in this treatise that all the references and Prophetic visions of God the Father that Jesus revealed and Jesus Christ Himself were attempts to ferment Christianity from Judaism and put the light of the candle lit by Christ under a bushel. The light of the candle must be put on the candlestick as to give light to all that are in the house" (Matthew 5:15) The work that the Father assigned to Jesus is also our work. "Let your light so shine before men, that they may see your good works, and glorify your Father which is in heaven." (Matthew 5:16) The Spirituality that Jesus introduced to the world is the new wine. Nobody ever produced or tasted that type of wine

9

before. That wine is that one promise from the Father for mankind and distributed freely to us to drink for a specific reason that I will reveal in this treatise.

This introductory revelation of Jesus here is a prologue into the mysteries of His exclusive intimate infinite relationship with God, the Father that Jesus revealed. "Therefore whosoever shall confess me before men, him will I confess also before my Father which is in heaven." (Matthew 10:32) He spoke with authority and acted with authority and was the voice and demonstrator of the works of His Father. Nobody had witnessed such wisdom and the power that Jesus displayed before. Jesus said on another occasion, "I thank thee, O Father, Lord of heaven and earth, because thou hast hid these things from the wise and prudent, and hast revealed them unto babes. Even so, Father: for so it seemed good in thy sight. All things are delivered unto me of my Father: and no man knoweth the Son, but the Father; neither knoweth any man the Father, save the Son, and he to whomsoever the Son will reveal him." (Matthew 11:25-27, Luke 10:21-22)

> *Ye are from beneath; I am from above; ye are of this world, I am not of this world.*
>
> ---Jesus (John 8:23)

The words of Jesus Christ in this prologue are like a door through which one begins to see Him beyond the boundaries of His humanity. To enter through that door into His Kingdom of God that came, is to enter into the mysteries Jesus's divinity. Jesus did not claim to be God the Father that manifested as a human being as portrayed by some overzealous Christian group. The knowledge of Jesus's Kingdom of God is very important. That knowledge is the only tool, that with certainty, reveals who Jesus Christ is, His Father and who we are. With reference to this His Kingdom,

Jesus revealed Himself as the Revealer (Mark 4:11-12); the Initiator (Matthew 11:4-5); the mediator (Matthew 12:28); and the Principal (Mark 4:3-20).

There are many Jesus's of sayings that gave insight on who He is. However, the real Jesus is revealed when the mysteries of His Kingdom and what happened at Golgotha are revealed. From His words that I have reproduced in the following texts, one can gain some knowledge of who is Jesus Christ.

The Father as the source of His power.

The Spirit of the Father in Jesus is the source of the power of His Kingdom of God.

> *The words that I speak to you are not mine but the Father who abides in me does the work.*

> ---John 14:10

His Lordship and divine authority

Jesus was taken to the pinnacle of the temple in Jerusalem, and Satan said to Him, "If You are the Son of God, throw Yourself down from here For it is written: 'He shall give His angels charge over you, to keep you and in their hands they shall bear you up, lest you dash your foot against a stone.' Jesus answered, "You shall not tempt the Lord your God." (Matthew 4:5–7)

> *And Jesus came and spoke unto them (the Apostles), saying, All power is given unto me in Heaven and in earth.*

> ---Matthew 28:18

> *All things are delivered unto me of my Father.*

> ---Matthew 11:27

The Father loved the Son, and hath given all things into his hand.

---John 3:35

For the Father judged no man, but hath committed all judgment unto the Son.

--- John 5:22

His knowledge of heavenly things

For the Father loved the Son, and showed him all things that himself doeth: and he will show him greater works than these that ye may marvel.

---John 5:20

And yet if I judge, my judgment is true: for I am not alone, but I and the Father that sent me.

---John 8:16

The voice of God, His Father with the Authority to reveal the truth about Father

Anybody who receives my commandment and keeps them will be one who loves me. And anybody who loves me will be loved by my Father, and I shall love him and show myself to him. If anybody loves me he will keep my words, and my Father will love him, and we shall come to him and make our home with him.

---John 14:21, 23

His authority to resurrect and give eternal life

For as the Father raised up the dead, and quickened them; even so the Son quickened whom he will.

---John 5:21

No man can come to me, except the Father which hath sent me draw him: and I will raise him up at the last day.

---John 6:44

Verily, verily, I say unto you, the hour is coming, and now is, when the dead shall hear the voice of the Son of God: and they that hear shall live.

---John 5:25-26

The way to know the Father

All things are delivered unto me of my Father: and no man knoweth the Son, but the Father; neither knoweth any man the Father, save the Son, and he to whomsoever the Son will reveal him.

---Matthew 11:27 Luke 10:22

If I do not the works of my Father, believe me not. But if I do, though you believe not me, believe the works; that you may know and believe that the Father is in me, and I in the Father.

—John 10:37–38

As obedient Son of His Father

Why did the Father choose Jesus and not another Spirit, to do the work? The Father chose the most trustworthy Spirit, on whom He had bestowed with omnipotent attributes from the beginning of time. He chose Jesus who always obeys His will.

I always do things that please Him.

---Jesus, John 8:29John 5:26

As the voice of the Father

For I have not spoken of myself; but the Father which sent me, he gave me a commandment, what I should say, and what I should speak.

---John 12:49

And I know that his commandment is life everlasting: whatsoever I speak therefore, even as the Father said unto me, so I speak.

---John 12:50

Demonstrator of the works of His Father

Jesus answered them, I told you, and ye believed not: the works that I do in my Father's name, they bear witness of me.

---John 10:25

Then answered Jesus and said unto them, Verily, verily, I say unto you, The Son can do nothing of himself, but what he seeth the Father do: for what things so ever he doeth, these also doeth the Son likewise. For the Father loved the Son, and showed him all things that himself doeth: and he will show him greater works than these that ye may marvel. For as the Father raised up the dead, and quickened them, even so the Son quickens whom He will.

---John 5:20-21

As the Executor of the will of His Father

For I came down from heaven, not to do mine own will, but the will of him that sent me.

---John 6:38

The will of the Father was not to drive the Romans away and restore the glory of Israel, but to fulfill that one promise of His Father to mankind that has something to do with creation and eternal life.

But I have greater witness than that of John: for the works which the Father hath given me to finish, the same works that I do bear witness of me, that the Father hath sent me.

---John 5:36

His intimate relationship with the Father

Jesus's experiences and His imageries of God, His Father, were unparalleled in any recorded human experience of God. The epitome of the life of Jesus is the mirror through which we see the deeper reflections of the portraits of the Father. During His earthly life, Jesus enjoyed an enviable unbroken bondage and experience with this God, His Father: "As the living Father had sent me, and I live by the Father." (John 6:57)

I am one that bears witness of myself, and the Father that sent me beareth witness of me.

---John 8:18

As the Father knoweth me, even so know I the Father.

---John 10:15

I and the Father are one.

---Jesus

Believest thou not that I am in the Father, and the Father in me? The words that I speak unto you I speak not of myself: but the Father that dwelleth in me, he doeth the works. Believe me that I am in the Father, and the Father in me: or else believe me for the very works' sake.

---John 14:10-11

The story of Jesus is not just the story of the 'historical Jesus. We must look beyond the physical image that was revealed two thousand years ago. To capture that shadow image, you must not look at Him with the lens of the Old Testament texts. We must look at Jesus with the lens of that one will of the Father for Jesus: the work that the Father gave to Jesus that He carried out with unbridled obedience to the Father. We must look at Jesus's Kingdom of God to find Him. He is inside that capsule that came down from His Father as a gift to mankind. If you do not believe in all the claims that Jesus made for Himself, as I have outlined above, then believe in that works that He did. The works that He did is the main subject of this treatise. The epiphany of the journey to eternal life-under the directorship of the new Gods, Jesus and His

Father-discussed in this treatise, centered on that commandment of His Father and Jesus's Kingdom of God. Jesus used Himself as an example to demonstrate the main task in that commandment and the great miracle of recreating Himself that revealed deeper mysteries of His Kingdom.

That the world may know that I love the Father; and as the Father gave me commandment, even so I do.

---John 14:31

CHAPTER 2

JESUS'S POLICY OF SILENCE AND SECRETS OF THE KINGDOM OF GOD

Because it is given unto you to know the mysteries of the Kingdom of heaven, but to them it is not given.

—Jesus to the Apostles. Matthew. 13: 11

Unto you it is given to know the mystery of the Kingdom, but unto them that are without, all these uttering are done in parables.

—Jesus to the Apostles. Mark 4:11

Silence was a major tool that Jesus used in the execution of His task. He considered it unnecessary to tell everything for the simple reason that His audience would not understand them. "If I have told you earthly things, and ye believe not, how shall ye believe, if I tell you of heavenly things?" (John 3:12) Jesus's Gospel of the Kingdom of God is indeed a book of hidden secrets and a compendium of mysteries of time and space that expanded to Golgotha and beyond. It forayed into the infinite realm of the spiritual universe and the divine nature of human souls that made the comprehension of the Kingdom that came difficult to comprehend. Many of its mysteries are still beyond full human understanding. Jesus completed His tasks for His Father and mankind and walked away without revealing in plain language the meaning of the kingdom of God and what was finished at Golgotha. Jesus maintained the policy of silence and secrecy on the real reason why the Father sent Him to the world.

How then can one break down the walls of the secrets and mysteries and pierce those coded illustrations and performances that would help one comprehend Jesus's Kingdom of God? How can we develop our spirituality so that we are able to project ourselves into the inscrutable mysteries of that Kingdom and see what it holds for us and what our tasks are so that we may be benefactors of it? Who can understand anything about the Kingdom of God that Jesus said was hidden in three measures of meal?

Whereunto shall I liken the kingdom of God? It is like leaven, which a woman took and hid in three measures of meal, till the whole was leaven.

—Luke 13:20–21

The woman hid the leaven in three measures of meal, why not in two or five measures? Recently, United State Department of Justice filed a motion seeking to compel Apple Inc. to unlock an encrypted phone. We cannot compel Jesus to unlock the encrypted messages of His Kingdom of God. To make such a demand today would be foolish because Jesus would quickly tell you to follow Him as to find the key to the mysteries of His Kingdom. My dear readers, I have unlocked the encrypted mysteries of the kingdom of God that Jesus hid in three measures of meal. To have knowledge of the mysteries of the Kingdom of God, you have to be patient 'till the whole (of the meal) was leaven. The three measures of meals represented the three grand stations on the trajectory of human creation as demonstrated by Jesus who used Himself as an example. A guided insight into what are in those three measures of meals, and how 'the whole was leaven' opens the floodgate to mysteries of Jesus's Kingdom of God, to who His Father is, to who Jesus is, to who we are, to why we are here and where we are going. The invitation of Jesus to the rich young ruler to follow Him, applies to us today. To fully understand what I have decoded from the parable of the leaven, we have to follow Jesus all the way to the end to hear His words and observe His works. This is the only way to understand the meaning of Jesus's Kingdom of God and its deep mysteries. You may ask; how do we develop spiritual eyes so that you may see in His Gospel what others fail to observe? How do we acquire spiritual perceptions that we may understand the meaning of it?

A man can receive nothing, except it be given him from heaven.

—John 3:27

Blessed are the eyes which see the things that you see. For I tell you that many prophets and kings have desired to see those things which you see, and have not seen them: and to hear those things which you hear, and have not heard them.

—Luke 10:23–24

Pray then, that the gates of this light may be opened too for thee; for these things can only be seen or known by those to whom God and His Christ have given understanding.

---Justin Martyre. A.D. 136

The more I look at what Jesus intentionally withheld and the mysteries of some of His utterances, many of which He would not reveal to the public, the more I am convinced He did it for a purpose. On many occasions, Jesus did not reveal the truth of what He was trying to convey to the people, instead Jesus hid the truth in parables, metaphors, parabolic utterances, and even in His miracles and instructions on how to pray to the Father. The characteristics of hidden secrets and mysteries seemed to be the platform on which He executed the Father's business. Jesus definitely refused openly to reveal who He was. When the chief priests and the scribes asked Jesus: "Art thou the Chris, tell us?" Jesus replied, "If I tell you, you will not believe." (Luke 22:67) What looked like a revelation of who He was, during His transfiguration and at His trial before the high priest Caiaphas was actually a revelation into more mysteries of His divine nature and power. He still withheld the revelation of the nature of the place where He came from and who He really was. Jesus said that nobody has heard the voice or seen the shape of His Father. However, would you not want to know more about the new God that Jesus called His Father and the place that is beyond the brightness of the sun?

Would you not want to know about the place where Jesus was all the time, before He made His appearance in Palestine? Would you not want to know what they use to monitor mankind that Jesus knew what Paul had planned to do in Damascus? Would you not want to know about the spiritual universe and how many spiritual kingdoms that are out there? Would you not want to know how the will of His Father is done in heaven? Would you not want to know the names of the spirits who, from the period of John, the Baptist, were trying to take the kingdom of God by force? Would you not want to know how many Gods are out there beyond our vision? Would you not want to know if Allah, the God worshipped by the Muslims is the same God as His Father? The big question is this: What is Jesus's Kingdom of God for us today? Why is it so important that we need to know its meaning and its mysteries? Would such knowledge help to control violence, wars, increasing refugee population, poverty, and instability in the world today? As of today, there is no solution to the Syrian war. The two great world leaders, President Obama and President Putin are Christians. They see the daily reports of horrific atrocities of that war. We all see them every day. We say nothing and we do nothing to stop that war. It is very sad that the two great world leaders-President Obama and President Putin, cannot as Christians, stop that war within twenty four hours. The United States Secretary of State, John Kerry, on February, 21. 2016 said; "No tactic such as being employed today will win the war in Syria." His mind set is on winning a war. The goal is not to win but stop the war, so that Syrians can go back to their country and rebuild. What is the tool in Jesus's Kingdom of God that we can use to help stop the war in Syria? If there is none, then all my efforts in writing this treatise would be useless. However, there are many tools in it that would fill up your house that everyone-the great world leaders, the world religious leaders, the Christians, the Jews, the Muslims, the Buddhists, and others-can use to stop the Syrian war within twenty four hours and all other conflicts in the world.

If the hidden secrets and mysteries coded in the Gospel of the Kingdom of God are decoded and revealed, all the spiritual tools would be displayed. We would begin to comprehend the common final glory that awaits all humans and our colossal task for its accomplishment. Perhaps the secrets and the mysteries of Jesus's words and deeds and the plan of the invisible God were not hidden from us but rather preserved for us for our own benefit. This is our moment. The time again is fulfilled. What was hidden has now 'come abroad.'

> *For there is nothing hid, which shall not be manifested; neither was anything kept secret, but it should come abroad.*

> --- Mark 4:22

The true meaning of the expressive language 'the Kingdom of God' as used by Jesus of Nazareth had remained elusive. The plethora of comparative parables and the symbolic parabolic expressions Jesus used in an attempt to convey the true meaning of the Kingdom of God is mind boggling. The mysteries of that Kingdom of God, that was kept secret since the world began, were revealed to the twelve holy apostles. "Because it given unto you to know the mysteries of the kingdom of heaven, but to them it is not given." (Matthew 13:11) Jesus even told them to put it in writing. He had told them, "But now, he that hath a purse, let him take it, and likewise, his script." (Luke 22:36) That script disappeared. I am not sure if they comprehended it well. Alternatively, it could be that Jesus instructed them to tell no one what was revealed to them about the kingdom of heaven. What if Jesus intentionally concealed the underlying aspects of what was hidden in the three measures of meal? Its comprehension would be impossible without the resurrection of Jesus. It would seem that the apostles did not reveal to anybody the meaning of the Kingdom of God as was revealed to them by Jesus. They did reveal elements of Jesus's Kingdom of God the way they understood them and manifested it by the way they lived during and after the death of Christ. Why then must Jesus hide from the public, the stupendous truth of the Good News of the Kingdom that He introduced to the world and revealed it only to the apostles? One of the reasons I outlined previously is that one has to seek and search for the truth. The most important reason is that if the truth was made easily available, they would not believe or even comprehend it. They would seek to destroy the source of such information. Jesus knew what would happen to Him if the news on how His Father is creating mankind, is revealed.

Give not that which is holy unto the dogs, neither cast ye your pearls before swine, lest they trample them upon their feet and turn again and rend you.

---Matthew. 7:6

Jesus was not deceived; He knows those who seeks the truth with spiritual eyes and listens to His words with spiritual ears. Jesus knows who has opened his or her heart in order to perceive, embrace, and develop the God-human in dwelling and experience. To those individuals-the chosen- the mysteries of the Kingdom of God were revealed. To reveal that truth on the Kingdom of God to those who would use it to disrupt what His Father and Himself designed for mankind-the creation of the spiritual mankind-is to give that which is holy to dogs and to cast one's pearls before swine.

Jesus resorted to the use of parables, not to reveal the meaning of the Kingdom of God, but as spiritual words that acted as a lens through which He conveyed to His audience, the nature of the Kingdom that came. However, most of the time, the audience and even the apostles could not comprehend the meaning of what looked like a simple story. "But without a parables spake He not unto them: and when they were alone, he expounded all things to His disciples." Mark 4:34

> *I thank thee O Father, Lord of heaven and earth, that thou hast hid these things from the wise and prudent and hast revealed them unto babes; even so Father, for it seemed good in thy sight.*

> ---Luke 10:21

When Jesus was alone with His apostles, He said to them privately, "Blessed are the eyes which see the things that you see. For I tell you that many prophets and kings have desired to see those things which you see and have not seen them; and to hear those things which you hear and have not heard them." (Luke10:23-24) What did those blessed eyes see that was hidden from others? Peter, James and John, saw the transfigured Jesus. He took them to a high mountain and, "was transfigured before them; and His face did shine as the sun, and his raiment was white as the snow." (Matthew 16:2) Jesus instructed them not to reveal what they saw till after His resurrection. What was it that was hidden from the wise and the prudent that the apostles heard? What was it that many prophets and kings desired to hear and that privilege was denied? What was the mystery of the Kingdom that Jesus shadowed in parables that was revealed to them and not to His audience? Did Jesus again give them the instruction not to reveal the mysteries of this Kingdom of God that came till after His resurrection? At that time, Jesus gave this instruction to them: "What I tell you in darkness that speak you in light; and what ye hear in the ear, that preach you upon the housetops. Fear them not therefore, for there is nothing covered that shall not be revealed; and hid that shall not be known." (Matthew 10:27, 26) The apostles and Paul proclaimed it and suffered the consequences. The Kingdom of God that came was one of the mysteries that were revealed to the apostles.

All things are delivered unto me of my father; and no man knoweth the Son, but the father; neither knoweth any man the Father, save the Son, and He to whomsoever the Son will reveal Him.

---Matthew 11:27

Jesus also surely revealed the Father and who He is to the apostles. However, this treatise at this stage is centered on the mysteries of the kingdom that were revealed to the apostles. The mystery revealed to the apostles was not how He was going to establish His Kingdom on Earth and crush evil activities or drive away the Romans and bring salvation to Israel. It is premature at this time to disclose what I recovered from the Gospel that was revealed to the apostles. Instead, I will discuss the grave consequences to Jesus Christ, His apostles, Paul and the early Christians when that information was revealed to the Jewish authorities and the Jewish people that believe in the authority of one God-Yahweh-as the only human creator and giver of eternal life. The mystery of the Kingdom of God that was revealed to the apostles became the lethal weapon that sent Jesus to Golgotha. What the Jewish authorities openly accused Jesus of, were not enough to disavow a true Israelite, condemn Him to death and hand Him over to their most hateful enemy-the Romans-to crucify.

Judas Iscariot was authorized by Jesus to release that information to the Jewish authorities. What was revealed by Judas to the Jewish authorities touched the essence and the core of their religion. They were angered beyond control. The Jewish authorities were not able to tolerate it. What Judas revealed to the Jewish authorities evoked such indignation that they immediately sent the mob with stakes and knives to arrest Jesus. Subsequently, He was condemned to death. It carried grave consequences for Judas also. Judas was subsequently found dead. The last place Judas was seen alive was in the Temple at

Jerusalem. The Jewish authorities vowed that no one with that information must be allowed to live.

After the ascension of Jesus Christ, the apostles who made attempts to reveal that information to the public as instructed by their Master were targeted, pursued from one city to another, and eventually killed. What the apostles revealed on the script on the Kingdom of God as was revealed to them by their Master, were destroyed. The apostle John escaped to the island of Patmos and took with him his scripts-known today as the Gospel of John. Mark, who gave the world the first text of the Gospel of Jesus, was not even an apostle. Perhaps he was fearful of his life and missed on purpose, to record the vital information on the kingdom of God that the apostles made public after the resurrection and ascension of their master. The other synoptic Gospels writers did the same.

> *This Jesus hath God raised, whereof we are witnesses. Therefore, being exalted by the right hand of God, that God had made that same Jesus, whom they crucified, both Lord and Christ.*

> ---Acts of the Apostles 2:32–36

The Pharisees, who formed the majority of the ruling party at the time of Christ, believed in the resurrection. The above proclamation that Jesus rose from the dead was not the reason for the beating and the imprisonment of the apostles in Jerusalem. James the brother of Jesus was killed. The apostles were pursued from one city to another and murdered. The blood of their Master was shed for the revelation of the truth to the Jewish authorities-through the authorized divine initiative of Judas Iscariot-on the Kingdom of God that came. Likewise the eleven apostles were counted as sheep for slaughter and killed for revealing publically what Jesus revealed to them in private on the mystery of the Kingdom, but instructed then to broadcast it after His resurrection. I believe that the disciple Stephen knew of that revealed mystery of the Kingdom. The Jews accused him of speaking blasphemous words against their God, but did not reveal the contents of those blasphemous words. Probably, it has something to do with what Jesus revealed to the apostles on the kingdom of God that the Jews considered offensive to their God and religion. Stephen was proclaiming that information among the people. The information carried the same grave consequence for Stephen like the other apostles. His fate was sealed when additionally, Stephen said, "Behold, I see the heaven opened, and the Son of man standing on the right hand of God." (Acts 7:56) They grabbed him and stoned him to death.

Saint Paul was a witness when Stephen was stoned and killed. He was a Pharisees, who also believed in resurrection. The fact that Jesus rose from the dead was not what troubled him. He condoned the action of the people that stoned Stephen not because Stephen said that he saw the risen Jesus sitting at the right hand of God. Paul was a learned man brought up under the renowned teacher Gamaliel, a doctor of the law. The fact that Paul was at Jerusalem when Stephen was stoned to death, showed that what Stephen was proclaiming on Jesus's Kingdom of God that came was the same thing the apostles and believers of Jesus were spreading everywhere. They must be stopped. He took it upon himself to participate in persecuting all preaching the words of Jesus Christ.

What words were they proclaiming that made Paul, the Hebrew of all Hebrews angry? I have devoted a whole chapter in this treatise on Paul and Jesus's Kingdom of God. The mystery of the Kingdom of God was revealed to Paul directly by the Spirit of Christ. Paul boasted of this direct communication in many of his epistles. That mystery fascinated him. For the proclamation of that revealed mystery of the kingdom of God to the Jews and Gentile, Paul was persecuted from one city to another by his people, as he pursued to spread the vital message on the Kingdom of God. The Jews were relentless. Paul was eventually beheaded in Rome. Again, they got the Romans to do the job.

Many of the early Christians were killed as they tried to spread the vital information on Jesus's Kingdom of God that came. When I started writing this treatise, I was frustrated with the apostles because they did not ask Jesus, Master, tell us, who are you, and what this Kingdom of God is. They did ask Him and He revealed Himself and the meaning of the kingdom to them. However, if Jesus had revealed who He was and the meaning of the Kingdom of God at the very beginning of His work to the public, you would have kissed the Father's business good-bye. The divine secret was endorsed by the Father and executed by Jesus for our own glory and for the planned work of our creation. At last, when the time was fulfilled-after His resurrection-the Son of man revealed who He was and allowed the apostles to proclaim publically what He revealed to then about the kingdom of God. This information was subsequently suppressed. We were forced to accept that Jesus and His apostles did not reveal the meaning of the Kingdom of God that came. Perhaps, they too were fearful of their lives.

However, Jesus's Kingdom of God that came is an irrepressible spiritual force. It was and still is the essential element in the human spiritual evolution of the human souls in their journey to eternal life. It is like, "the seed which a man cast into the ground, and should sleep, and rise night and day, and the seed should spring and grow up, he knoweth not how. For the earth bringeth forth fruit of herself; first the blade, then the ear, after that the full corn in the ear. But when the fruit is brought forth, immediately he putteth in the sickle, because the harvest is come."

(Mark 4:26-29) When what Jesus revealed to His apostles on the Kingdom of God that came, is revealed in this treatise, it may be a shock to you. You will understand why Jesus was condemned to death and anyone that publically proclaimed it was killed by the Jews.

By the time the crucible Christianity made its appearance to the world during the reign of Emperor Constantine, who legalized Christianity in the Roman Empire in AD 313, what was revealed to the apostles and subsequently to Paul on the Kingdom of God disappeared from its manifesto or at best became so fragmented. That vital information disappeared from the Gospel of Jesus that was presented to us. The new wine was craftily mixed with the old wine and the new cloth was used to patch up the torn old clothes. Perhaps, the Christian leaders at that time allowed it to happen as to protect themselves, as the proclamation of the revealed information on the Kingdom of God, carried with it, lethal consequences. Christianity at that time refused to drink anymore from this cup of martyrdom. The conflict with Judaism looked on the surface to have ended. What seem to be liberation of Christianity from the Jewish influence and antagonism was really the abandonment of the implementation and acknowledgment of the revealed mysteries of the Kingdom of God that the Jews considered offensive to their religion. The human consequences of this changed policy will be discussed later. However, what Jesus revealed to the apostles in private on the kingdom of God-and told to use it as the framework to continue the works of His Father-is like "the light that shined in darkness and the darkness comprehended it not" because it was hidden from us. This privileged vital information on the Kingdom of God is the first act of Jesus's words and works that I will discuss in this treatise. The revealed mysteries of Jesus's

Kingdom of God propelled the words and the works of Jesus to new dimensions. Despite the reluctance of the Christianity that developed after the period of persecution and martyrdom, to proclaim what Jesus revealed to the apostles, Jesus's Kingdom of God that came-not the Kingdom of this world or a physical place-increased and expanded worldwide, bearing with it the core elements that Jesus brought down from the Father for the earthly phase of human creation.

> *But we speak the wisdom of God in a mystery, even the hidden wisdom, which God ordained before the world unto our glory...... But the natural man receives not the things of the Spirit of God: for they are foolishness unto him: neither can he know them, because they are spiritually discerned.*

1 Corinthians 2:7, 14

> *Blessed is he, whosoever shall not be offended in me.*

---Matthew 11:6

CHAPTER 3

THE NAKED TRUTH OF JESUS'S KINGDOM OF GOD

The Gospel literature revealed two forms of the Kingdom of God: 1. The Kingdom of God with many mansions. (John 14:2) 2. The Kingdom of God that came (Matthew 12:28) and within you (Luke 17:21) The Kingdom of God with many mansions is the boundless spiritual realm where God and His angels reside. According to the Christian belief, it is the final destination for all humans. It is also referred to as Paradise. Jesus promised the thief who was also crucified at the same time that he will be with Him in Paradise. Jesus prayed for His disciple to be with Him in that place to see His glory: "Father, I will that they also, whom you have given me, be with me where I am; that they may behold my glory, which you have given me for you loved me before the foundation of the world" (John 17:24) For Mary Magdalene, she must not touch Him till after He presents Himself to His Father: "Touch me not; for I am not yet ascended to my Father" Jesus. The place where Jesus went to present Himself is the Spiritual Realm that was before the foundation of the earth. It is still in existence today. It is an everlasting Kingdom of His Father. Jesus did not reveal much about that Kingdom. If He had done so, no one would have believed Him. Jesus told Nicodemus, "If I have told you earthly things, and ye believe not, how shall ye believe, if I tell you of heavenly things?" (John 3:12)

This epiphany is centered on the Kingdom of God that came with power and is "within us." It is that Kingdom that came with power in Palestine and some people at that time witnessed the manifestation of its power.

The time is fulfilled, and the Kingdom of God is at hand: repent ye, and believe in the Gospel.

---Mark 1:15

But if I by the finger of God cast out devils, no doubt the Kingdom of God is come upon you.

--- Luke 11:20, Matthew 12:28

Verily I say unto you, that there be some of them that stand here, which shall not taste death till they have seen the Kingdom of God come with power.---Mark 9:1

Jesus started His mission with the proclamation that the Kingdom of God was imminent. Today, if presented to us at that stage of His mission, we would call Him a dreamer. His audience was mesmerized by the power of the kingdom that came. Jesus introduced something that was new to the world: a new Kingdom of God that came. He began His mission with the proclamation that the Kingdom of God was within us and demonstrated the power of it with His miracles. The Kingdom of

God that came was not the arrival of God's rule on earth. God rules all the time. It was not necessary for Jesus to come down and remind us that God rules all the Time. It is not a place where God reigns with power and authority, forcing His will on mankind. It is not an earthly or future spiritual Kingdom to be established on earth. To get a grasp on the meaning of the Kingdom of God and its mysteries, we have to know why His Father sent Him to the world. We would like to know if He brought any gift for mankind from His Father and if so, what that gift is?

> *If God were your Father, ye would love me, for I proceeded forth and came from God, neither came I of myself, but He sent me.*

> John 8:42

> *I came down from heaven not to do mine own will, but the will of Him that sent me.*

> ---John 6:38

> *Then said they unto him, Where is thy Father? Jesus answered, Ye neither know me, nor my Father: if ye had known me, ye should have known my Father also.*

> ---John 8:38

Jesus repeatedly said that He came down from heaven and that His Father sent him to the world. If you were present at that time, would you not, like the Jews ask Him who is this Father, where is this His Father and why did He send him to the world? Today, would you not want to know if that Father is the same God that spoke to Moses and what He brought down from His Father for us?

Jesus left a well grounded impression-I will reveal in this treatise-that His Father is not the same God that spoke to Moses. This disclosure and separation of the two Gods makes it easy to understand the meaning of Jesus's Kingdom of God.

The works that His Father sent Jesus to accomplish, took Him all the way to Golgotha-where He was crucified-and beyond. The triumphant glory of that work was showcased at His resurrection. The work was rekindled and continued again in on the day of the Pentecost. It is still going on today. It is not possible to know the meaning of Jesus's Kingdom of God and its mysteries by the review of Old Testaments literature or by in dept analysis of His parables on the Kingdom of God. On many occasions, Jesus simply encouraged people to follow Him. To grasp the meaning of the Kingdom that came, you have to follow Jesus to Golgotha and find out what He said that was 'finished' just before He died on the cross. To have a glimpse into its mysteries, you have to know what Jesus's resurrection means to mankind and what it revealed about the work He was sent here to do by His Father.

Jesus was born into this world as a human being. His Father planned it that way. Jesus exercised that choice to be born a human being. He could have chosen to come down as a Spirit as was revealed at His transfiguration and at His resurrection. But He chose to come down as one of us. To grasp the meaning of Jesus's Kingdom of God, its objectives and goals, we have to know why Jesus chose to be clothed with human qualities. What is revealed in many passages of His Gospel is that the Spirit of His Father was also in Jesus Christ. "The words that I speak to you are not mine but the Father who abides in me does the work." (John 14:10) The Spirit of that Father led Jesus to the wilderness to be tempted by Satan. That Spirit directed all His words and deeds. "Verily, I say unto you, The Son can do nothing of Himself, but what He sees the Father do for what things soever He doeth, these also doeth the Son likewise. For the Father loves the Son, and showed Him all things that Himself doeth; and will show Him greater works than these, that you may marvel." (John 5:19–20) That Spirit powered all the miracles of miracles of Jesus. It was the power behind His resurrection and the promised gift that came on the day of the Pentecost. In essence, the Kingdom of God that came is the *activated* Spirit of the Father in Jesus's human soul. This is Jesus's Kingdom of God.

> *But if I by the finger of God cast out devils, no doubt the Kingdom of God is come upon you.*

--- Luke 11:20, Matthew 12:28

All the mysteries of that Jesus's Kingdom of God are hidden in one miracle: Jesus's everlasting miracle of the earthly stages of human creation. The last scene of that miracle was showcased on the day of Pentecost!

Jesus heard the voice of that His Father. He prayed to that Spirit, obeyed its commands. "For I have not spoken of myself, but the Father which sent me, He gave me commandment, what I should say and what I should speak. I know His commandment is life everlasting; whatever I speak therefore, even as the Father said unto me, so I speak." (John 12:49-50) Jesus manifested the power of that Spirit of His Father by performing many miracles.

What then is the Kingdom of God within us?

Jesus said that He came down from heaven with this Spirit of the Father to do His will and work. Jesus was born into this world as a human being to show us that we can have the same Spirit of the Father in our human souls, put it into action, do great works, even greater works than He did and harness all its blessings. To understand where we fit in and how we can get it, first we want to know what the will of God is? What type of work did Jesus accomplish for the Father? To get a deeper understanding of our Kingdom of

God that is within us, two most important questions are: how did Jesus get that Spirit from the Father and what did He do with that Spirit? I have set the platforms that if we find the answers, would give us guided insights to the meaning of Jesus's Kingdom of God and the proclaimed Kingdom of God within us and the connecting link between them.

How and when Jesus got the Spirit from His Father will remain an inscrutable mystery. If it is revealed to us, of what use will it be to us. The most important question now is: What is the use of that Spirit to us? If all that Jesus did with that Spirit was to show its power by performing miracles and resurrected Himself, then it is of no value to us. Perhaps our inability to retrieve from the words and works of Jesus from the Gospel the value of that Spirit to us in this 21st century, is the reason why many of our children are flocking to the business world to enrich them and build earthly treasures that will make them happy. Perhaps, it is the same lack of knowledge of what Jesus did with the Spirit that He got from His Father that have over the last two thousand years, prompted the erection of expensive Cathedrals in preparation for the second coming of Christ and planted the seed of ignorance in the knowledge of what Christ proclaimed, prescribed and demonstrated.

The Spirit of God, the Father of Jesus Christ, is the living life itself. Without it, the humans you see with your eyes will one day vanish like some dinosaurs did in the past. With the Spirit of that God, you will live forever, even after death. This is the life Jesus came to give, not just to the apostles but to all mankind. Two thousand years ago, when the time was fulfilled, a new era dawned for humanity- a new era for the fulfillment of the Father's promise for mankind. Jesus was sent down by our Father to fulfill that promise. He was equipped with the Spirit of that Father for that task for mankind.

A complete survey of the words and deeds of Jesus Christ revealed that there is only one promise of the Father to us. Jesus tactfully revealed that promise of the Father as the Kingdom of God that He proclaimed. "Seek ye the Kingdom of God. For it is your Father's good pleasure to give you the Kingdom." Jesus. (Luke12:31, 32) Jesus went about the cities and villages with His apostles, proclaiming that promise. He worked and died for the fulfillment of that promise. After His resurrection, Jesus continued to preach and disseminate information on that Kingdom of God that the Father promised. He sent all His apostles to all parts of the world to reveal this promise of the Father to mankind. On the fiftieth day after His crucifixion, on the day of Pentecost, the Father sent down again the Spirit of the risen Christ (the Holy Spirit), also known as the Comforter or the Holy Ghost, for the same purpose as was revealed by Jesus before His ascension. That promise was completely misunderstood as was evidenced by the gross misrepresentation of Jesus's Kingdom of God as an earthly Kingdom. It was substituted by another false promise, the second coming of Christ, when He will establish His spiritual Kingdom on earth.

What then is Jesus's Kingdom of God within us and why we need it? The answer comes from what Jesus did with the Spirit of the Father in Him. Jesus used the power of it in performing miracles that included His epic miracle of human creation. Jesus spiritualized the human souls with it as revealed what He did with it in the parable of the Sower. (Matthew 13:3-18; Mark 4:3-20) The field in that parable is the human heart. The Sower is Christ. The seed is the Spirit of the Father in Him. Moving forward, I will henceforth refer to the Spirit of the Father in Jesus Christ as the Spirit of Christ. Jesus was the Mediator appointed by His Father to freely implant His Spirit to all human souls who are willing to receive it. The proclaimed Kingdom of God within us is *activated* Jesus's Kingdom of God that is within us. This is activated the Spirit of Christ within human souls! The Spirit of Christ is the Spirit of the Father in Him. To be endowed with the Spirit of the

Father is not enough. Water in a cup is of no value if we refuse to drink it as to sustain life. Likewise, a human soul as a component of the Kingdom is of no value if it is inactive. An inactive human soul cannot leverage the power of the Kingdom as to sustain it and guide it as it moves along the earthly stages of human creation. It would not be able to manifest any of its divine elements as demonstrated by the life examples of Christ. This inactivity as a member of Jesus's Kingdom of God was portrayed in His parable of the Talents. (Matthew 25:14-30; Luke 19:12-27) The servant in that parable who received one talent and did nothing with it represent the human soul who entered into Jesus's Kingdom of God and refused to obey the will and commandments of the Father. The human soul as a component in the Kingdom of God is a priceless element to Jesus and His Father. The Spirit of the Father in Jesus Christ is also a priceless divine element in that Kingdom of God. There are four types of this Kingdom of God as was revealed by Jesus in the parable of the Sower.

1. The Kingdom of God in action within human souls. The human soul here is the good ground that brought forth fruits. This is the true Kingdom of God. Today, the people who possess this true Kingdom of God opened their doors and offered hospitality to the refugees who fled from their countries because of war. Many in the world who posses it are doing everything in their power to alleviate human sufferings and serve mankind. They use tolerance, peaceful methods instead of war to settle conflicts. Their services to mankind are not polarized. Most importantly, they have no hatred in their hearts.
2. The dead souls without the Kingdom of God. In this Kingdom, the human soul refused to accept the Spirit of Christ-the seed fell by the way side. Today, they represent the people who put up barbed wire fences to prevent the

refugees from getting into their countries. They operate on the platforms of hatred, injustice and selfishness. Human souls without Jesus's Kingdom of God cannot make that journey of life by themselves.

3. The ostentatious Kingdom of God. The human soul accepted the Spirit of Christ but got distracted by evil activities-hatred, selfishness, injustice, racism, inability to love and forgive others, jealousy and inability to obey the will and commandments of the Father and Christ-and lost it. They preach the life of Christ but live another way of life. This type of Kingdom belongs to people who seek earthly powers and glory. Their souls are like stony grounds without much earth. This is a false Kingdom of God.

4. The temporary Kingdom of God. The human soul accepted the Spirit of Christ and manifested it for some time. However, the care of the world, the quest for earthly treasures and the 'deceitfulness of riches,' made the bond with the Spirit of Christ impossible. Their souls are like grounds with thorns. They do not have the spirit of the true Kingdom of God proclaimed by Jesus. Today, you see them everywhere. They take all they can from everybody because they are in the position to do so, and give nothing back.

Jesus's Kingdom of God that He revealed to the apostles in private is the Spirit of the Father in Him-the Spirit of Christ-in their souls. While He was with them Jesus bestowed that Spirit to them. Jesus called that His Spirit, the Spirit of the truth.

You know Him (my Spirit), *He* (my Spirit) *shall live in you and shall be in you.* Jesus said to his apostles.

--- John14:17

40

The next question is this; why do we need it? Why we need it was given a practical demonstration by Jesus. First, He demonstrated the power of it, an indication that we have that power if we have the Kingdom of God. Second, with that Kingdom in Him, Jesus used the creative trajectory that passed through death and resurrection to recreate Him. Here on this earth, we are placed as incomplete created human beings. We are unconscious of it and unaware of the earthly phase of the evolutionary process. We need Jesus's Kingdom of God to complete our creative process. With the coming of the Kingdom of God-the entry of the Spirit of Jesus into the world- a new phase in the human creative activities with His Spirit commenced. It was a defining moment in human history when His Father's design for humanity unfolded. Those who are broadened by the knowledge of God's promise and stay on the narrow path of the Father-Jesus Christ human creative trajectory pass on to a fuller authentic life. Third, the divine elements inside Jesus's Kingdom of God, also ingrained on our souls who entered into it as part of His Kingdom, were made manifest and demonstrated by the epitome of the earthly life of Christ. To enter into that Kingdom today, and have the experience of it, is to manifest those divine elements and live like Christ. In essence, Jesus's Kingdom of God within us, is not just the Spirit of Christ in human souls. It is the Spirit of Christ in action within the human souls, manifesting its creative power, love for His Father, love for one another, love for the enemy, mercy, compassion, forgiveness, justice and obedience to the commandments of the Father and Jesus Christ. Jesus revealed all the mysteries of that Kingdom in human soul, its creative power, the revelation of His Father, and Himself, in His epic miracle of the earthly stages of human creation by His death and resurrection. Jesus used Himself as a human model. *This is the naked truth of Jesus's Kingdom of God and its mysteries*

Jesus's Kingdom of God was the promised gift that the Father gave to mankind for a specified purpose: the completion of earthly stages of the creation of human life to its full spiritual expression. "Come, ye blessed of my Father; inherit the Kingdom prepared for you from the foundation of the world. (Matthew 25:34) However, the completion of this creative process depends on the activities of the human soul in Jesus's Kingdom of God within us. Jesus lived actively the life of the Spirit of His Father in action within His soul to show us that we can do it also. It is for this reason the He came down as a human being. He came down from heaven with this Spirit of the Father and gave it to us to live the life of the Spirit of His Father. Jesus used Himself as a model to exemplify that way of life. The second promise of the Father is again like the first promise. The Father will send in the name of Jesus Christ 'the Comforter, which is the Holy Ghost. (John 14:26). The Holy Spirit is a brand name of the Spirit of God in the glorified Spirit of the risen Christ. The promised gift sets the framework for Jesus Christ to continue the works of His Father. What I have pointed now in this part of the treatise, will set you on the same platform-the Father-Jesus Christ-mankind creative trajectory-that I used to analyze and re-examine what I recovered from the words and works of Jesus Christ on the Kingdom of God, His death and resurrection.

Jesus's Kingdom of God is the Paradise of the human soul. It is not a new unexpected interruption in the history of human creation. It is a proclamation and demonstration of what has been going on from the beginning of human creation before Jesus came. It would continue uninterrupted to the end of time as determined by God the Father of Jesus. The association of the Spirit of the Father and Christ with human souls has been going on since the beginning of creation. But what they use it for, was hidden from everyone. The reason why the Father and Jesus Christ chose not to reveal themselves before Jesus came and the reason why they chose to reveal Jesus's Kingdom of God only when 'the time was fulfilled' would remain an inscrutable mystery. Perhaps, at the right time in human evolution, the Father and Jesus decided to reveal themselves and demonstrate to us who are creating mankind and to make the earthly stages of creation easy for us to understand.

The flagship of the Kingdom of God that came was the Spirit of Christ. It carries with it eternal life giving creative power-the promised gift from the Father-that kindled all human souls, propelling them to their final destiny. Jesus, as His custom was used parables, metaphors and figurative expressions-as shown below-as tools to expound and illuminate His Spirit-the Spirit of the Father in Him. The gift-His Spirit-to human souls was presented symbolically and metaphorically by Jesus Christ as:

The Living water.

Jesus answered and said unto her, If you know the gift of God, and who it is that said to you, Give me to drink; you would have asked of him, and he would have given you living water.

---John 4:10

But whosoever drinks of the water that I shall give him shall never thirst; but the water that I shall give him shall be in him a well of water springing up into everlasting life.

---John 4:14

The Wind.

The wind blows where it listed, and you hear the sound thereof, but cannot tell from where it comes and where it goes; so is every one that is born of the Spirit.

---John 3:8

The Bread of Life and the Manna from heaven.

I am that Bread of life. This is the bread which cometh down from heaven, that a man may eat thereof, and not die. I am the living bread which came down from heaven: if any man eats of this bread, he shall live forever: and the bread that I will give is my flesh, which I will give for the life of the world.

---John 6:48, 50-51

My Blood and Flesh.

Then Jesus said unto them, Verily, verily, I say unto you, except you eat the flesh of the Son of man, and drink his blood, ye have no life in you. Whoso eats my flesh, and drinks my blood, hath eternal life; and I will raise him up at the last day. He that eats my flesh and drinks my blood dwells in me, and I in him.

---John 6:53-54, 56

The Yoke

Come unto me, all ye that labor and are heavy laden, and I will give you rest. Take my yoke upon you, and learn of me; for I am meek and lowly in heart: and ye shall find rest unto your souls. For my yoke is easy, and my burden is light.

---Matthew 11:28-30)

Fire

> *I am come to send fire on the earth; and what will I, if it be already kindled?*

> ---Luke 12:49

The Salt

> *For every one shall be salted with fire, and every sacrifice shall be salted with salt. Salt is good: but if the salt has lost his saltiness, wherewith will ye season it? Have salt in yourselves, and have peace one with another."*

> ---Mark 9:49-50

The implication of this new reinterpretation of the kingdom of God as exclusively the Spirit of Christ in action within human souls takes a quantum leap from our complete reliance on a God that we do not really know-for everything, to a God that Jesus called His Father who endowed Him with His Spirit and with divine authority to do all His works. Without any reservation, Jesus made this divine authority from His Father public. "All things are delivered unto me of my Father." (Matthew 11:27) This same Father "gave Him power over all flesh, that He should give eternal life to many" (John 17:2) Perhaps this prompted Jesus to tell the people, "I and my Father are one" and told the apostle Thomas, "If you have seen Me, you have seen the Father." Jesus never claimed to be the Father and insisted that "the Father is greater than I."

The Jewish authorities knew that Jesus not only personified the new Kingdom of God that He introduced with Himself and His power, but also incorporated into it the Spirit of the new God that He called His Father. What they refused to accept, was that a son of a carpenter, untutored in their religion, who, associated Himself with the poor, the alcoholics and the sinners, was the power behind the control of the new Kingdom of God that Jesus introduced. They did not believe Him. Some thought Jesus was insane and possessed with the Devil. The Jews believe that human life and eternal life was of their God to give and not this Father that Jesus revealed and that any Kingdom of God must be as envisioned by the Prophet Daniel. It must be under the reign and control of Yahweh alone. When the meaning and the mysteries of that Jesus's Kingdom of God, revealed to the apostles secretly, was revealed to the Jewish leaders by Judas Iscariot-authorized to do so by Christ-that information became the lethal weapon to Jesus, Judas Iscariot and subsequently to many of His apostles.

The power of Jesus's Kingdom of God manifested in all His miracles. "But if I by the finger of God cast out devils, no doubt the Kingdom of God is come upon you." (Luke 11:20; Matthew 12:28) Jesus's message to John the Baptist was this:

> *Go and show John again those things which ye do hear and see: the blind receive their sight, and the lame walk, the lepers are cleansed, and the deaf hear, the dead are raised up, and the poor have the gospel (of the Kingdom) preached to them.*
>
> ---Matthew 11:4-5

The platform for all the miracles was Jesus's Kingdom of God. The Christians and their leaders and the theologians who were not able to give a meaningful interpretation of Jesus's kingdom of God agreed on one thing: that Jesus personified that Kingdom of God. That personification extended to His death and resurrection. Jesus's Kingdom of God was in all His words and works. It holds the key to all the words and works of Christ.

What has this Kingdom of God to do with us today? Jesus's kingdom of God is everywhere. We have first to know what it is. Inside its capsule are three powerful Spirit-the Spirit of the Father, the Spirit of Christ and the Human spirit. Human spirit is something that the Lord made and time forgot. We live today as in the past to glorify the body. The quest for the human glory made us spiritless as evidenced by human atrocities. Human beings could never attain to full created spiritual forms, without our full participation in the process of creation. This is our free will. Without the willingness of the human spirits, Jesus could not have been able to perform any of the healing miracles. The spiritual capabilities of the human souls in the Kingdom of God when revealed showed that we can do all that Jesus did and with the same modus operandi He used by the manifestation of the divine nature of the Kingdom-forgiveness that extends to the enemy, compassion, mercy, unselfishness, love for the Father and mankind, service to humanity including the refugees, care of the poor, and absolute trust in His Father. The human spirit with the Spirit in its creative trajectory to eternal life must pass through the divine essence of this Kingdom of God. The human must be rekindled-born again with the Spirit of Christ-for the actualization of eternal life. This is the hidden treasure of this gift of the Spirit of Christ-the gift of His kingdom. That was the bread that came from the Father.

The power of invisible Spirit of the Father in Him enabled Jesus to perform miracles and cast out evil spirits. The Kingdom of God is not a movement that seeks national leaders and followers or the worship of our ancestral spirits or graven images of any form. In its equation, there is nothing materialistic in its formula that could be used as a measure of successful materialistic life. This Kingdom of God is divine in its origin and purpose; iridescent with a deep spiritual enthusiasm in its manifestation, heavenward to a higher infinite human destiny in its direction. It contains the mind of God, the way to eternal life, the light to direct you to His Father and the spiritual tools to use as weapons to love and stop killing one another. It is the true light which lights on everyone who comes into the world. It is the compass that directs, protects and guides you to the glorious destiny: the infinite trinity of your souls with the Father and Jesus Christ.

As ages pass, some recognize the glorious destiny and the great vastness of Jesus's Kingdom of God in the little space within our hearts. They see the greatness of God's plan for all humanity for this boundless Kingdom and recognize it is the right thing to seek after the objectives of the Kingdom and the righteousness of God. They utilize the spiritual tools in the Gospel of the Kingdom for their participation in the miracle of the human stages of human creation and for the advancement of their spiritual evolution and control of evil activities in the world. They comprehend the task for its accomplishment: use of negotiation to avoid wars, the determination to avoid racism and religious conflicts, hard work, suffering, sorrow, despair, loneliness, trust, compassion, justice, truth, reconciliation, repentance, love, charity, empathy, obedience of the will of God, believe in the Father and in Jesus Christ, love of all mankind, protection of the earth's environment, patient in tribulation, and humility and forgiveness in victory, the zeal to help poor nations and not to steal from them, and the devotion to preach Christianity as prescribed, proclaimed and demonstrated by Christ. Human beings never really transcend to the marked level of the desired or planned spiritual evolutionary status for entry into Jesus's Kingdom of God, until their hearts are broken. Those who are deepened or broadened by their experience of the Kingdom of God, rise triumphantly from their spiritual immaturity to a fuller destiny in the union with the Father and Jesus Christ. Along this critical pathway lays the kingdom of God-the Spirit of Christ in human souls. The 'Christ in me' was the core element in Pauline spirituality as he tried to alert both Jews and the Gentiles of this divine gift in him and the power of it. Paul was born again with the Spirit of Christ.

The core element and the framework of all the words and the works of Jesus centered on this special gift of His Spirit to human souls, the protection of the spiritualized souls and the works He did with that Spirit for His Father. The works that He did for His Father with His Spirit is the new creation of human life to its ultimate end. For us this is the intrinsic value of Jesus's Kingdom of God that came and is within us. God was involved in it in the past, and is involved in it now and in the future. Jesus Christ was involved in it from the beginning, before Abraham, and still involved in it now and in the future. Abraham, Isaac, Jacob, Moses, the wise men, the Prophets of Israel and John the Baptist all benefitted from it. All the apostles, the Jews-including the people that condemned Him to death-and the Romans that crucified Him, benefitted from it. Paul, Stephen and the martyrs in the crucible period of Christianity were involved and benefitted from it. The Jewish Diaspora, who mounted intense mortal opposition to the works of the Kingdom of God, benefitted from it. Today, the people of the Greco-Roman Empire are in it. They benefitted from it and will continue to do so. Today we are all in it and are benefitting from it and will continue to do so in the future, if you believe in the Father and Jesus Christ and in that one promise of the Father for mankind that was executed by Jesus Christ. Our children and all future generation will benefit from it. The dead will benefit from it-some already did-and will continue to do so.

The consequences of lack of true religious knowledge are obvious to everyone today: hatred and killing of one another under various facades. It is the main factor that has caused division among all that ever lived on this planet in the past, today and will be in future if we do nothing. The fundamental drive is not so much as the quest to please a God but the quest to control human activities by religious leaders. The politicians in leadership do the same. On our current trajectory as shown by what is happening in the world today, clearly shows that we lack of knowledge of who we are, why we are here and Jesus's Kingdom of God and its mysteries. On this trajectory, mankind would not be able to inherit the Kingdom prepared for us from the foundation of the world or harness the gift from God, the Father of Jesus, for our full expression of life here and in the spiritual world.

And blessed is he, whosoever shall not be offended in me.

---Jesus. Matthew 11:6

CHAPTER 4

OBJECTIVES AND GOALS OF THE KINGDOM OF GOD

*My doctrine is not mine, but His that sent me. If any man
will do His will, he shall know of the doctrine, whether it
be of God or whether I speak of myself.*

—John 7:16

The doctrine in Jesus's Kingdom of God is the doctrine that God delivered to us through Jesus Christ. Jesus and His Father had all the powers and human resources for a successful outcome of what Jesus came to accomplish. The Father controlled and directed all things: "For I have not spoken of myself; but the Father who sent me, He gave me a commandment what I should say and what I shall speak. And I know that His commandment is life everlasting. Therefore, whatever I speak, just as the Father has told me, so I speak." (John 12:49–5) Mankind devoid of the knowledge of that plan must be guided and tutored as to gain that vital knowledge and be a participant of that plan. That plan is still active today and is unstoppable, proceeding at a speed that is ordained by God. The lack of knowledge of the plan puts humans in utter darkness of the Father's plan for creation and the purpose why we are here. The Father has never looked away from any human being. We have never been separated from Him.

First, Jesus focused on the core messages of the Kingdom of God that came. To give a meaning to the Kingdom of God without the sermons being an essential part of it is to present a dead Kingdom. It would defeat the objectives and goals of the Kingdom. The human souls in the Kingdom would be inactive, unable to produce fruit worthy of eternal life as was portrayed in the parable of the Barren Fig tree. (Luke 13:6-9) Jesus made all efforts for this not to happen. Jesus outlined what we must do to be active participants in the activities of the Kingdom. First we must sell all our earthly possessions, distribute the proceeds to the poor, and then follow Him to the Father. That command of yesterday is still the same today and will be in future. Our ability, in His name to, harness the power of the Kingdom, "cast out devils, speak with new tongues, take up serpents and drink any deadly thing and it shall not hurt us, and lay hands on the sick and they shall recover," (Mark 16:17-18) depends on our obedience of that commandment. It was a commandment that penetrates the frontiers of earthly possessions, loves for the poor and the enemy, and believes in Jesus and His Father that sent Him. It is a responsibility that binds us to His Kingdom of God. Our colossal task is to work for perfection of our souls so that we may receive the gift of the Spirit of God and be active participants in the Kingdom. "Be perfect even as the Father is perfect." (Matthew 5:48)

If we are to have knowledge of what we must do for our glory and the fulfillment of the Father's promise for mankind, all we have to do is to look at Jesus's unprecedented way of life, His belief in His Father, His sermons and love for His Father and all mankind. All these were Jesus's attempts not only to direct people to His Kingdom of God but also to instruct them on how to achieve the objectives and goals of the Kingdom. Jesus made Himself the epitome of mercy, love, compassion, forgiveness, peace, and justice. Jesus was a trusted, loyal, and obedient Mediator for God's plan. He labored relentlessly in a systematic manner that guaranteed glory for humanity and victory for God. We too must work with Jesus so we can share the joy that was set before us and rejoice together as was written; "Behold, I say unto you, lift up your eyes and look at the fields, for they are already white for harvest! And he who reaps receives wages, and gathers fruits for eternal life, that both he who sows and he who reaps may rejoice together." (John 4:35–36) The fields are the souls of the inhabitants of earth. Our souls are ready for spiritualization in preparation for eternal life. To "gather fruits for eternal life" is to be active participants with Jesus in the Kingdom of God for our everlasting glory. This is the will of Jesus, which is a duplication of the will of God.

Salt is good: but if the salt has lost his savour, wherewith shall it be seasoned? It is neither fit for the land, nor yet for the dunghill; but men cast it out. He that hath ears to hear let him hear.

---Luke 14:34-35

Human soul 'salted' with the Spirit of God is good and fit for the Kingdom of God. But if the human soul that lost the divine elements of that bond by refusing to live and manifest the nature of that Kingdom as prescribed, proclaimed and demonstrated by Christ, is a dead soul. However we are given many opportunities to redeem our souls and participate in the Kingdom activities as was illustrated again in the parable of the Barren fig tree.

He spoke also this parable; a certain man had a fig tree planted in his vineyard; and he came and sought fruit thereon, and found none. Then said he unto the dresser of his vineyard, Behold, these three years I come seeking fruit on this fig tree, and find none: cut it down; why cumbered it the ground? And he answering said unto him, Lord, let it alone this year also, till I shall dig about it, and dung it: And if it bear fruit, well: and if not, then after that thou shall cut it down.

---Luke 13:6-9

You would think that if the Master comes back again and found no fruit on the tree, that he would command the tree to be cut down. Jesus would not give the instruction for the tree to be cut down if the man again promises to 'dig about it and dung it' again. Perhaps it would take seventy times seven years before Christ would finally give up and cut the tree. The message here is repentance and forgiveness. Our participation in the activities of the Kingdom is so important to Jesus that he is willing to forgive all who are making real efforts to enter into that Kingdom and be active participants in their creation. The importance of this was illuminated when Jesus said to His disciples, "if he (thy brother) trespasses against you seven times in a day, and seven times in a day turn again to you, saying, I repent, you should forgive him." (Luke 17:1-4) The ground for this is that it is what He learned from His Father. It is what His Father does. It is the will of His Father.

Jesus refused to reveal the objectives of His Kingdom of God to the public in a plain language they could understand. He resorted to sermons, instructions on how to pray and obey the will and commandments of His Father. Jesus left no room for people to ask Him why they must listen to Him, instead He warned that:

Whosoever cometh to me, and heareth my sayings, and doeth them, I will show you to whom he is like: He is like a man which built an house, and digged deep, and laid the foundation on a rock: and when the flood arose, the stream beat vehemently upon that house, and could not shake it: for it was founded upon a rock. But he that heareth, and doeth not, is like a man that without a foundation built a house upon the earth; against which the stream did beat vehemently, and immediately it fell; and the ruin of that house was great.

---Luke 47-49

Why were all these instructions important to Jesus? Do we need them today? Some look at Jesus today as one who disrupted the glorious history of mankind where the winner takes all the prizes. Jesus introduced the concept that there must be no earthly winners. The invisible Father and Jesus Christ are always nearby and see everything we do. Jesus insisted that, "the very hairs of your head are all numbered." (Matthew 10:30) What Jesus did was to place us on the platform of complete dependence on Him and the Father on all our activities, including the very human life we enjoy. Jesus outlined the rewards of the winners in His Beatitudes. (Matthew 5:3-12) To illuminate what Jesus was up to and why He went through cities and villages preaching on the Kingdom of God, we have to look at the objectives and goals of that Kingdom that came.

Objectives of Jesus's Kingdom of God

Reveal the benefits of the Kingdom
Encourage people and provide free opportunities for admission into that Kingdom
Reduce the number of people who would reject it
Plan rewards for people who would accept it
Inspire people to participate in the earthly stages of their creation
How to harness the power of the Kingdom and use it in our creative process

Train the apostles on leadership with essential tools for the demonstration of the Kingdom
Help prepare everyone on how to be active participants in His Father's plan
Direct all humans to the path that leads to His Father
Methods on how to develop partnership with Him and His Father
Spiritualize human souls with the Spirit of the Father
Control the obstacles to the spiritualization of human souls
Demonstration of the methods of the earthly stages of human creation
Silence and control other Gods
Reveal the nature and power of His Father
Disseminate all information on the Kingdom to the world.
Provide pitfall to avoid in the dissemination of the knowledge
Promote its growth by globalization of all the three stages of His epic miracle of human creation.

What Jesus used to highlight objectives of the Kingdom?

Demonstration of its power by performing miracles
The epitome of His life
His words: the parables, the metaphors, the Beatitudes, the Sermon on the Mount, the Lord's Prayer and two great commandments of God
His temptation by Satan

Goals of the Jesus's Kingdom of God

Complete the demonstration of the earthly stages of human creation
Demonstrate the prototype of the fully created spiritual human being

Enthrone His Father as the universal God
Control of the influence of other Gods on human minds
Reveal His Father and Himself as Creators
Reveal to mankind, how to be participants in their own creation as spiritual beings
Reveal the knowledge of eternal life: the divine Trinity of the created spiritual human souls with the Father and Himself

Jesus's divine directives are not mousetraps that He used to intimidate us to enter into His kingdom, but catalysts for the bond that would orient and direct us to participate in our creation. They are spiritual in origin. They are the directives from His Father, delivered to mankind through Him.

Come, ye blessed of my Father; inherit the Kingdom prepared for you from the foundation of the world.

---Matthew 25:34

For what is, a man profited, if he shall gain the whole world, and lose his own soul? Or what shall a man give in exchange for his soul?

—Matthew 16:27

Jesus's Kingdom of God that is within us, when revealed in any age, translated into any language, or disclosed under any religious names and symbols, guides the human soul to a fuller destiny, to a life hidden in God, the Creator, through Jesus Christ. "For it pleased the Father that in Him (Jesus Christ) should all fullness dwell." (Colossians 3:19) It gave humanity access to the knowledge of the invisible God, to the awareness of what is life. It educated the human souls so that they could develop and advance to the highest evolutionary level and participate in what the Father and Jesus Christ are creating. It is the power that propelled the fully created human spirits to a divine union with the Father and Jesus Christ. This is the glory and the blessings of the Kingdom of God that came.

Blessed is He who came in the name of the Lord.

---Matthew 23:39

CHAPTER 5
JESUS' PARABLES OF THE KINGDOM OF GOD

Why do you speak unto them in parables?

—*Mark. 13:10*

Jesus revealed in private, some but not all of the hidden secrets in the parables to the apostles. "And with many such parables He spoke the words to them as they were able to hear it. But without a parable He did not speak to them. And when they (the apostles) were alone, He explained all things to His disciples." (Mark 4:33) The parables of Jesus were earthly stories with deep heavenly connotations, relating to activities kept secret from the foundation of the world. The only way Jesus could tell us of heavenly things is to relate them to human life, nature, and everyday human activities. What looked like a bizarre and enigmatic methodology that Jesus used to disseminate the nature of the Kingdom of God, was indeed a well-crafted *modus operandi* that revealed:

The inseparable link of the Kingdom with human souls and the Spirit of His Father
The objectives of the kingdom
The goal and the human benefits of the Kingdom that came
The importance of vital knowledge of the Kingdom that came with power
His infinite control of that Kingdom.
The irrefutable connection of the Kingdom of God with human life
The indisputable reliance, sustenance and survival of human life on the Kingdom of God

A scrutinized examination of Jesus's parable of the kingdom of God revealed that it is bound with Him, His Father who sent Him, the human souls and the earthly phase of the human creative trajectory. Jesus also used the parables of the kingdom of God, not to reveal what it is to the public, but to illuminate the nature of it, the mighty works it would accomplish, the obstacles it will encounter, the rewards and the blessings for mankind.

How shall I compare the parables of Jesus of Nazareth, in what comparison shall I compare them with? The illumination of the galaxy by the heavenly stars is comparable to the illumination of the Gospel of the Kingdom of God by His parables. Jesus' parables are the stars of His Kingdom of God. Jesus' profound use of daily human activities and of the humans' natural environment captivated His audience and made the divine instructions easy to remember. However, the complexity of the parables surfaced when humans attempted to interpret them, thus prompting the apostles to ask Jesus on many occasions to interpret them. "And when He [Jesus] was alone, they that were about Him with the twelve asked of him of the parable [of the Sower]" (Mark 4:10) In reply, Jesus said unto them: "Know you not this parable? And how then will you know all parables?"

Our misinterpretation of the meaning of the Kingdom of God made it impossible for us to grasp the meaning of the parables associated with it. With what shall I compare the parables of Jesus? They are like the story of the poet Homer's Proteus, the old man of the sea, who could assume any shape he chose. When he was seized by Menelaus and his men as they attempted to learn the way to their homeland: First he shifted into a great bearded lion and then a serpent-- a panther--a ramping wild boar-- a torrent of water--a tree with soaring branch tops-- but we held on for dear life, braving it out until, at last, that quick-change artist, the old wizard, began to weary of all this and burst out into rapid-fire questions: 'Which god, Menelaus, conspired with you to trap me in ambush? Seize me against my will? What on earth do you want?' You know, old man,' I countered now. 'Why put me off with questions? Here I am, cooped up on an island far too long, with no way out of it, none that I can find, while my spirit ebbs away. But you tell *me*--you immortals know it all—which one of you blocks my way here, keeps me from my voyage? How can I cross the swarming sea and reach home at last? *The Odyssey by Homer.* Translated by Robert Fagles. Page 138-139 Penguin Books

To 'reach home'-to decipher the meaning of the parables of Jesus-the 'immortal who know it all' must help us. It is for the same reason that the apostles always asked Jesus to explain the meaning of the parables to them, that they too may understand the heavenly things, as they prepare themselves to preach the Kingdom of God In cities and villages of Palestine. As His custom was, Jesus crafted the parables in a mosaic pattern, not for the purpose of confusing His audience but by searching with the spiritual eye, one may find the hidden truth. "Ask, and it shall be given you; seek, and ye shall find, knock, and it shall be opened unto you. For every one that asks, receive, and he that seeks, find, and to him that knocks it shall be opened." (Matthew.7:7, 8)

It has been more than two thousand years since these stories were written, but if we remove the parables that Jesus expounded to His disciples, theologians have given different interpretations to the rest of the parables. The parables of Jesus are the greatest stories ever told. We love those stories and yet the spiritual truth behind the stories is hidden. He knew the reason why He did not even attempt to explain publically any of the others. To have done so would be like casting one of His spiritual weaponry to dogs and swine who would trample on it. The effects of the parables of Jesus on human consciousness are inexhaustible. They are like an energizer to the hearts. They bring joy of remembrance to Jesus who said He came to proclaim the kingdom of God. They are a light to our souls and bring forth all that is new and old for God-Jesus-Human Spirit creative trajectory and experience. Of all the spiritual weaponries Jesus used for the revelation of His Father and His Father's holy purposes in the staged human creation, His parables would be given the Summa Cum Laude status and a valedictorian on a grading scale level. Except for the spiritual events at Golgotha and the pragmatic Lord's Prayer, nothing came close to it, nay, not even the Beatitudes. The parables are like double jeopardy. Not only are they spiritual weaponry mankind must use as a guide for God-Jesus Christ-Human Spirit creative process and experience, but they are, like lamp posts in a spiritual garden. The spiritual garden in this context is the kingdom of God that came.

The light from the lamp posts would help you find other spiritual weaponries you must use for eternal life. Everyone that has heard the stories of the parables of Jesus's Kingdom of God never forgets them. They are like the stories of the spiritual events at Golgotha. Once you hear such stories, you will never behave as though you never heard of them. But the most intriguing aspect of these stories is that whenever they are told to those who heard them before; their excitement is the same as if they had never heard them before. Never before had stories remained in the consciousness of humans as the stories of these parables. The entire heavenly and earthly inhabitants are represented in the stories of Jesus' parables of the Kingdom. The Father that sent Him is in those stories. It is very interesting that one finds himself, his family, his nation, his religious group, and almost all human activities in the stories.

Why then must Jesus hide the stupendous truth of the Good News of the Kingdom that He introduced to the world in parables? One of the reasons I outlined previously is that one has to seek and search for the truth. Another reason is that if the truth was made easily available, they would not believe or even comprehend it. Jesus knew what would happen to Him if the truth is revealed prematurely.

"Give not that which is holy unto the dogs, neither cast ye your pearls before swine, lest they trample them upon their feet and turn again and rend you."

Matthew. 7:6

Jesus was not deceived; He knows those who seek the truth with spiritual eyes and listens to His words with spiritual ears would eventually know the meaning of His Kingdom of God. Jesus knew those who opened their hearts in order to perceive, embrace, and develop the God-human in dwelling and experience. To those individuals-the chosen- the mysteries of the Kingdom of God are revealed: "Unto you it is given to know the mystery of the kingdom of God." (Mark 4:11); and "when they were alone, he expounded all things to His disciples." (Mark 4:34) However, outside His inner circle of disciples, all these things are portrayed in parables. To reveal those truths through parables to those that would not use it to allow his Father and Himself to do what was designed for mankind-the creation of the spiritual mankind-is to give that which is holy to dogs and to cast one's pearls before swine. The parables of

Jesus are spiritual words that acted as a lens through which Jesus conveyed to His audience, not only the nature of the Kingdom that came but also His divine authority in-charge of the entity

The Gospel records revealed that only two of the parables were explained to the disciples by Jesus: the parable of the Sower (Matthew 13:3-23; Mk 4:2-20; Luke 8:4-15) and the parable of the Wheat and Tares (Matthew 13:24-30). We are not sure if the narratives Jesus used to reveal His parables are fictitious or real, but it is reasonable to assume that He "who was before Abraham" and was "before the foundation of the world" had witnessed all the stories He used among the previous human generations that existed millions, or even billions, of years ago or from His experience with them since the first stage in human creation. Some of the stories, when projected as the background of the contemporary human activities, look familiar. The past treatment of slaves, the current treatment of migrant workers (in the United States, Great Britain, Europe, and China), the migrant refugees, the attitudes of privileged children, the businesses of buying and selling illegal drugs, the greed of men and women, the quest for earthly wealth, the activities of our religious leaders, the obstacles to the Kingdom of God, and the neglect for the accumulation of spiritual treasures can all be seen in the stories of Jesus's parable of the Kingdom.

As I searched the Gospel, it became obvious to me that behind the veiled presentation of all of Jesus' parables of the Kingdom of God, are well-crafted, divine revelations and instructions that lead to eternal life. This life is made possible by the gift from the Father. I must reiterate again, that human creation is not a one day event, but a multi-phased process that is still going on now. The parables of the Kingdom of God will be comprehended when viewed against the back ground of the staged God- human creative process. When viewed with the lens of Jesus Christ that brought down our gift from the Father that was used in the demonstration of the earthly phase of that process, the parables would become guiding lights that shines into Jesus's Kingdom of God, revealing its mysteries. These are what I will reveal in this treatise, not only to make all parables of the kingdom of God comprehensible but to reveal the incredible human potentials in those parables.

There is not yet a categorization of the parables of the Kingdom that revealed a comprehensive conception of the revealed truth hidden in those parables that correlated with His message on the Kingdom of God. There are overlaps in the truth revealed in Jesus' parables. The interpretations of many of the parables are problematic. "Take heed what you hear; the measure you give will be the measure you get." (Matthew 4:24) One must be very careful in deciphering the truth that is hidden in the parables. However, I am confident that I recovered the blueprint from the records of the words and deeds of Jesus that made the etymology of parables of the Kingdom of God comprehensible. Many of the parables are repetitions of the same truths in different settings and frameworks targeted towards different audiences. The truth revealed in the parables of the great pearl and of the hidden treasure is the same. The truth when revealed as narrated in the parables of the kingdom is the one lifetime grand ambition for the acquisition of that gift from the Father through Jesus Christ for the staged God-human creative activities and experience that leads to eternal life: the divine trinity of the human soul with the Spirit of the Father and Jesus Christ.

The ancient Greek philosopher Aristotle was once considered the master of metaphors. The metaphors in Jesus' parables of the Kingdom, granted Him the honor of being the universal Grandmaster of metaphors. A parable of Jesus may contain more than one metaphor and characteristics of allegories. The crafted revelations and divine instructions in Jesus' parables transcend complete human comprehension. The parables of the Kingdom of God as preached by Jesus may contain features unrelated to the Kingdom of God but essential to the revelation of the veiled spiritual truth of the Kingdom. The complexity of Jesus' parables of the Kingdom makes it difficult to categorize or group them. However, the deep spiritual truths revealed in those parables are easy to understand when we categorize all of them as a single spiritual weapon that Jesus used to reveal the true message of the Gospel of the Kingdom of God within us and to immortalize His Gospel as well. How can one forget the stories of Lazarus sitting on the lap of Abraham, the Good Samaritan, the Prodigal Son, the wise and foolish Virgins, the lost sheep, the Sower, and the house built on a rock and on sand? You will, I hope, begin to comprehend why Jesus would not teach without parables as was written: "And with many such parables spake He the word unto them, as they were able to hear it. But without a parable, He spake not unto them." (Mark 4:33)

A survey of Jesus's parables of the Kingdom, when revealed, will show the followings:

The nature of His Father and His design for mankind
The divine nature of Jesus and His role in human creation
The personalized human participation in the earthly phase of creation
The nature and the power of the Kingdom
Who we are, why we are here and the intrinsic value of human life
The Kingdom of God that came and is within us
The destiny of our immortal created human spirit
How we are to live and enter into Jesus's Kingdom of God
The irrepressible growth of the Kingdom

"Men do not light a lamp and put it under a bushel, but on a stand, and it gives light to all in the house."

Matthew 5:15; Mark 4:21; Luke 11:33.

Jesus's parables of the Kingdom of God are the lamp posts in His house. Here, the house represents the Kingdom of God that came without observation. Let the light from His parables help you find the spiritual weapons in His Gospel that you may know God, develop the God-human experience, and allow Him to continue creating you through Jesus Christ. There is hope that the hidden truth in all the parables of Jesus, will all be made manifest one day, as was written: "For there is nothing hid, which shall not be manifested; neither was anything kept secret, but that it should come abroad." Mark 4:22.

> *These things have I spoken unto you in proverbs; but the time cometh, then I shall no more speak unto you in proverbs, but shall show you plainly the Father.*

> ---John 16:25.

Jesus would ask us today, "What is the Kingdom of God in your heart like?" To what should I compare the forgotten Spirits of Christ in your hearts? It has to be like a mustard seed that a man took and tossed into his garden. It will grew and became a tree, and the birds of the sky roosted in its branches [modified from Luke 13:18-20]. The man that took the mustard seed and tossed it into his garden was Jesus Christ. To understand more of that parable of the Kingdom, and all other parables of the Kingdom, you must sell all your possessions and distribute to the poor and follow Jesus to be a spectator when He unwraps what was hidden in three measures of meals. You must be ready for the journey with no shoes, one coat, no money, no back-pack, no water and no food. God, the Father, sent Jesus to the world through Joseph, a carpenter, and Mary, his wife. They were poor. Jesus, their son could not rely on them for money for His mission. When asked to pay tax, Jesus did not send James, His brother to Nazareth to get money from His parents or from his sisters and brothers. God, His Father, did not make any monetary allowance. The Father sent Jesus down with His Spirit. The mighty works Jesus did with the Spirit of the Father in Him-the Spirit of Christ-is the main subject of this treatise.

He that reads let him understand.

---Jesus

CHAPTER 6

MANIFESTATIONS OF THE POWER OF THE KINGDOM OF GOD

*And they were all amazed, and spoke among themselves,
saying, what a word is this! For with authority and power
He commanded the unclean spirit and they came out.*

—*Luke 4:36*

*Verily, I say unto you. He that believes on me, the works
that I do shall he do also; and greater works than these
shall he do.*

—*John 14:12*

The Father's promise is to give us the Kingdom of God that Jesus proclaimed. His will is for us to believe in Jesus Christ, whom He sent to the world. This belief in Christ is rooted in what He proclaimed, prescribed for mankind and demonstrated in the epic miracle of the earthly stages of human creation. The Father's plan is to reveal to mankind these earthly stages of human creation. Jesus was given full authority and power by the Father to do that work. Why is this power of Jesus's Kingdom of God important to us? The answer is simple: we need it not only as sustenance for survival but also as the core element in our transcendental transformation to new creatures-the spiritual human beings. In essence, we need it in our earthly stages of human creation to be fully created. The power of the Kingdom of God must be reviewed and interpreted on these unified platforms. From these we can form an idea why Jesus went about the villages and cities in Palestine demonstrating the power of the kingdom that came. Those demonstrations ranged from-miraculous healings, feeding five thousand people with only five loaves of bread and two fishes, walking on water, calming and controlling the storm, turning water into wine-to the resurrection of Lazarus and Himself. Jesus performed so many healing miracles that the people-the Pharisees and the doctors of law also-were so impressed that they assumed that "the power of the Lord was present to heal them." (Luke 5:17)

The best demonstration of the power of His kingdom before His death was the miraculous healing story in the Gospel of the woman who had menorrhagia, for duration of twelve years. (Mark 5:25-34) She had gone to many doctors for treatment, but they were not able to cure her. She had "spent all that she had, and was nothing better, but rather grew worse." Then when she heard of Jesus, she joined the multitude and got to a position behind Jesus and touched His garment. For she said to herself: "If I may touch but His clothes, I shall be cured." The woman was immediately healed. Jesus knew that part of His healing power had emanated from Him and asked;

Who touched me?

The woman told Jesus the truth that she did.

Where did Jesus get this power to perform miracles? Did Jesus get it from Satan during His Satanic temptation in the wilderness? Satan boasted of his power and offered to share it with Jesus.

Again, the Devil takes him up into an exceeding high mountain, and showed him all the kingdoms of world, in a moment of time; And the Devil said unto him, "All this power will I give thee, and the glory of them; for that is delivered unto me; and to whomsoever I will I give it. If thou therefore will fall down and worship me." Then said Jesus unto him, "Get thee behind me, Satan, Satan: for it is written, Thou shall worship the Lord thy God, and him only shall thou serve.

—Luke 4:5-8

The power of Jesus Christ was not from Satan. The gross misunderstanding of the source of Jesus's power confused many of His people. Some of them suggested He got His healing power from Beelzebub, the prince of devils. Jesus, on His own part had repeatedly told His audience that the Spirit of His Father was in Him. That Spirit of Father in Jesus Christ is the source of the Power. "But if I with the finger of God cast out devils, no doubt the kingdom of God is come upon you." (Luke 11:20)

Metaphorically, the Spirit of God in Him was presented as the finger of God. At first, Jesus announced that the kingdom of God was near, and then sent out His apostles to villages and cities to proclaim that the Kingdom of God was at hand. By the time they came back, travelling from one village to another, Jesus was ready to show-by demonstrating the power of the Kingdom that came-by turning water into wine in Cana of Galilee. (John 2:1-11) The performance of miracles was a confirmation that the Spirit of the Father was in Jesus. We do not know when such event took place. All I can tell you is that when Jesus said that the kingdom of God was at hand, He was sure it would come. It came with power and authority. The promise of the Father-the gift of the kingdom of God to mankind-was fulfilled. Jesus Christ in all His works and words presented His Spirit as a prototype of the Spirit of His Father. Jesus used the gift of the Spirit of the Father that came to Him as His Spirit of the Kingdom of God He proclaimed, to execute the works of His Father. "Believest thou not that I am in the Father, and the Father in me? The words that I speak unto you I speak not of myself: but the Father that dwelleth in me, he doeth the works." (John 14:10)

Jesus shared His power with the apostles and the seventy men He sent out to preach the Kingdom of God ant to heal the sick.

Then he called His disciples together and gave them power and authority over all devils, and to cure diseases. And he sent them to preach the kingdom of God and to heal the sick.

---Luke 9:1-2

The apostles obeyed their Master's command. This time they went about the villages and cities preaching –not only of the kingdom of God-but demonstrating the power of it. When the seventy returned, they said to Jesus: "Lord, even the devils are subject unto us through thy name." (Luke 10:17) How Jesus transferred His power to those people is an inscrutable mystery. The apostles knew that they had that power and had experience of it.

The apostles had obeyed His will; they were obedient to His laws and commandments. They had received His Spirit and manifested its power. In return, God had granted them heavenly privileges to enter the heavenly glory. While on earth they have the power as the angels do in heaven. The twelve apostles, the seventy men that were sent out to preach the Gospel and Paul, were few of the familiar names we know. Jesus's final instruction to the apostles before His ascension was this: "go, preach, saying, The Kingdom of God is at hand. Heal the sick, cleanse the lepers, raise the dead, cast out devils, freely give" (Matt 10: 8.) For the twelve blessed holy men, Jesus had already erected His Kingdom in their hearts. "Lo the Kingdom of God is within you". With sublime obedience, the apostles carried out the command of their Master with joy and gladness. They had cast out devils, and healed many that were sick. The hostility of the Samaritans prompted some of the apostles-James and John-to ask Jesus to authorize them to call down fire from heaven to destroy them. Jesus replied:"Ye know not what manner of spirit ye are of." (Luke 9:54-55)

Mankind is more than what you see and can touch. Human being is a living spirit, evolving to gain power and full expression of what the Father promised mankind. The sharing of the power of Christ was intended for all mankind. All transportation vehicles need fuel as to move from one place to another station. The satellite needs fuel for its launching into the space. Human soul needs as its fuel-the power of the Spirit of Christ-as to move to creative trajectory and gain the full power and the divine nature of that work of God that Jesus came to execute.

The demonstrations of the power of the kingdom of God by Jesus were not to show how powerful He is. Whenever the power of the kingdom of God is discussed, we automatically think of the miracles of Christ. Jesus manifested the power of the Kingdom that He proclaimed in many ways. Even His death and resurrection were manifestations of the power of that Kingdom. Jesus used it for multiple purposes:

As a platform that attracted thousands of people to hear the words of life: the words He got from His Father

The words that I speak unto you, they are spirit, and they are life.

---John 6:63

As a platform to demonstrate the power that His Father gave Him

Go and show John again those things which you do hear and see: the blind receive their sight, and the lame walk, the lepers are cleansed, and the deaf hear, the dead are raised up, and the poor have the Gospel preached to them." Jesus said to the two disciples sent to Him by John, the Baptist.

---Matthew 11:4-5

As evidence that the Father sent him to the world

The works which the Father hath given me to finish, the same works that I do, bear witness that the Father hath sent me.

---John 5:36

I told you, and ye believed not; the works that I do in my Father's name, they bear witness of me.

---John 10:25

To show love and compassion for the sick.

To convince people to believe in Him. During many of the healing miracles, Jesus usually asks them; do you believe that I am able to do this? In His home town-Nazareth- he was not able to perform many miracles because they did not believe in Him,

That whosoever believeth in him should not perish, but have eternal life. For God so loved the world, that he gave his only begotten Son, that whosoever believeth in him should not perish, but have everlasting life.

---John 3:15-16

The Jews had asked Jesus to tell them plainly if He is the Christ. Jesus replied: "I told you and ye believed not; the works I do in my Father's name, they bear witness of me. But ye believed not."

---John 10:24-2

To show that the sharing of His power was intended for all mankind.

Verily, verily, I say unto you, He that believeth on me, the works that I do shall he do also; and greater works than these shall he do."

---John 14:12

As the framework to gather people together and disseminate information on the nature and the will of His Father, the works the Father gave Him to do, and to reveal what are human life and His own nature

As a platform to assemble people from all nations for the invisible transfer of the Spirit that He got from the Father to individuals who believe in Him and in His Father.

He that hath my commandments, and kept them, he it is that loved me: and he that loved me shall be loved of my Father, and I will love him, and will manifest myself to him.

---John 14:21

Jesus answered and said unto him, if a man loves me, he will keep my words: and my Father will love him, and we will come unto him, and make our abode with him.

---John 14:23

To convince people believe in His Father by the demonstration of the real works the Father had given Him to execute: spiritualization of mankind and recreation of Himself through His death and resurrection. That was the theatrical drama that Jesus staged in a ubiquitous modus operandi. Jesus was the Director and the principal Actor. Other actors and the actresses were real. That event-the once upon a time historical vital event, is what I recovered from the Gospel and portrayed it as Jesus's everlasting miracle of human creation. Jesus used Himself as a model. The epic miracle was grossly misunderstood by Jesus's audience and the Jewish authorities. Today we are still trying to understand it and its application to the human life.

To reveal His power and authority.

To reveal His Father as the Creator and the only true God

To reveal that He is also a Lord of resurrection, and also a Creator. This was the evidence that Jesus provided by using Himself as a model in His everlasting miracle of the earthly stages of human creation.

To show that He can forgive sins. It was not necessary for Him to die as to be able to forgive sins.

To reveal the power of the human spirit

Ye know not what manner of spirit ye are of." Jesus said to the apostles. Luke 9:55 *Verily, I say unto you. He that believes on me, the works that I do shall he do also; and greater works than these shall he do.*

---John 14:12

Throughout the Gospel there were records of protean manifestations from people who received the Spirit of Jesus Christ. How is it that today very few people are capable of demonstrating that power of Jesus's Kingdom of God? First, we have to ask, what is in this power of Jesus Kingdom of God that He used in performing miracles? That power guided Him in the exhibition of perfected earthly life, and propelled Him along the road of abuse, disgrace, insults and scorn, to Golgotha. It uploaded and lifted Him to the cross, and then released Him on the third day after the gruesome ordeal. Second, we have to take the veil of the power of that Kingdom of God to see what is behind it. Paul called it Charity.

Though I speak with the tongues of men and of angels, and have not charity, I am become as sounding brass, or a tinkling cymbal. And though I have the gift of prophecy, and understand all mysteries, and all knowledge; and though I have all faith, so that I could remove mountains, and have not charity, I am nothing. And though I bestow all my goods to feed the poor, and though I give my body to be burned, and have not charity, it profited me nothing. Charity suffereth long, and is kind; charity envied not; charity vaunted not itself, is not puffed up. Does not behave itself unseemly, seeks not her own, is not easily provoked, thinks of no evil; Rejoices not in iniquity, but rejoices in the truth. Bears all things, believes all things, hopes in all things, and endures all things. Charity never fails: but whether there be prophecies, they shall fail; whether there be tongues, they shall cease; whether there be knowledge, it shall vanish away. For we know in part, and we prophesy in part. But when that which is perfect is come, then that which is in part shall be done away. When I was a child, I spoke as a child; I understood as a child, I thought as a child: but when I became a man, I put away childish things. For now we see through a glass, darkly; but then face to face: now I know in part; but then shall I know even as also I am known. And now abides faith, hope, charity, these three; but the greatest of these is charity.

---Paul 1 Corinthians 13:1-13

That s charity is love. It was the dying command of Christ to His apostles:

> *As the Father hath loved me, so have I loved you: continue ye in my love. If ye keep my commandments, ye shall abide in my love; even as I have kept my Father's commandments, and abide in his love. These things have I spoken unto you, that my joy might remain in you, and that your joy might be full. This is my commandment, that ye love one another, as I have loved you. Greater love hath no man than this: that a man lay down his life for his friends.*

---Jesus. John 15:9-13

When the veil of the power of Jesus's Kingdom of God is taken off, what is revealed is the infinite love of the Father and Jesus for all mankind. It is the love of the Father for Jesus and the love of Jesus for the Father. It is the love that energized and inspired Him to lay down His life for His friends. It is the love that cried out in a triumphant outburst from the cross: "It is finished." It is the love that moved and invigorated Jesus to come to this planet earth. It is that love that was decoded and prescribed to us by Christ as the two great commandments.

> *Thou shall love the Lord thy God with all thy heart, and with all thy soul, and with all thy mind. This is the first and great commandment. And the second is like unto it, Thou shall love thy neighbor as thyself.*

---Matthew 22:37-39

It is the unconditional love that is expected from us at all times under all conditions.

But love you your enemies, and do good, and lend, hoping for nothing again; and your reward shall be great, and ye shall be the children of the Highest: for he is kind unto the unthankful and to the evil. Be ye therefore merciful, as your Father also is merciful.

---Jesus. Luke 6:35-36

That love was behind what people witnessed in His works and heard in His words. It was the love that sustained Christ on the cross. It is for that infinite love that He is still interacting with mankind today and would continue to do so in the future. Today, we try to make disciples of all nations by performing miracles with the power of the Kingdom of God. We put up television shows curing children crippled with polio and restoring the sights of people blinded with glaucoma with the power of the Kingdom. We make people millionaires with the power of the Kingdom of God. These are not miracles or manifestations of the power of the Kingdom. How can we manifest it when our hearts are filled with hatred, racial injustice, greed at the expense of others and leave no room for that love as outlined in the doctrines of Jesus's Kingdom of God? Of all the divine elements- compassion, love, mercy, justice, forgiveness-in the invisible capsule of the power of the Kingdom of God, love occupies a strategic indispensible position in it. How can we manifest the power of the Kingdom of God when mankind chose the nuclear power and weapons of mass destructions that are killing what the Father and Jesus Christ are creating? How can mankind manifest that power when we have placed so many obstacles on the trajectory of Jesus's Kingdom of God in its attempt to achieve its goal? Many do not understand the meaning of Jesus's kingdom of God. How can we manifest the power of what we do not know that is within us? How can we manifest the power when we have refused to enter into that Kingdom and participate in our creation? There were some who for the last two thousand years manifested the power of that kingdom before they died. There are still many in the present world, even among your neighbors, who will not taste death until they see the kingdom come with power. Jesus wants everyone to be able to perform miracles. "Verily, I say unto you. He that believes on me, the works that I do shall he do also; and greater works than these shall he do." (John 14:12)

What Jesus accomplished is irrepressible. It would continue to grow. However, many have to take this journey with Jesus all the way to Golgotha and beyond to learn of Him. We have to-if you are willing- grab the power of His Spirit to gain full spiritual expression of what the Father promised and what Jesus proclaimed, prescribed and demonstrated in His everlasting miracle of the earthly stages of human creation. Good luck!

CHAPTER 7

AN OPEN INVITATION: A TASTE OF JESUS'S KINGDOM OF GOD

The parable of the great feast

Then said he unto him, a certain man made a great supper, and bade many: And sent his servant at supper time to say to them that were bidden, come; for all things are now ready. And they all with one consent began to make excuse. The first said unto him, I have bought a piece of ground, and I must needs go and see it: I pray thee have me excused. And another said I have bought five yoke of oxen, and I go to prove them: I pray thee have me excused. And another said, I have married a wife, and therefore I cannot come. So that servant came, and showed his lord these things. Then the master of the house being angry said to his servant, Go out quickly into the streets and lanes of the city, and bring in hither the poor, and the maimed, and the halt, and the blind. And the servant said, Lord, it is done as thou hast commanded, and yet there is room. And the lord said unto the servant, Go out into the highways and hedges, and compel them to come in, that my house may be filled. For I say unto you, that none of those men which were bidden shall taste of my supper.

---Luke 14:16-24; Matthew 22:1-10

In the above parable, 'my supper' is the metaphor for Jesus's Spirit. In another instance, Jesus called it "His flesh", "His blood" and "the bread that came down from heaven." Jesus had said to His listeners; "Verily, verily, I say unto you, except ye eat the flesh of the Son of man, and drink his blood, ye have no life in you. Whoso eats my flesh, and drinketh my blood, hath eternal life; and I will raise him up at the last day. For my flesh is meat indeed, and my blood is drink indeed. He that eateth my flesh, and drinketh my blood, dwelleth in me, and I in him. As the living Father hath sent me, and I live by the Father: so he that eateth me, even he shall live by me. This is that bread which came down from heaven: not as your fathers did eat manna, and are dead: he that eateth of this bread shall live forever." (John 6: 53-58) Do not confuse the bread and the wine offered to the apostles during the Last Supper or the wine and bread offered during the Eucharist, as the Spirit of Christ, or as something that would make us to obtain eternal life.

How can we get the Spirit of Christ? Why do we need it? What can we do with it? If we get that His Spirit, how do we know that we have it? The Spirit of Christ in human souls, as I have revealed in this treatise is Jesus's kingdom of God in action. The spiritual evolution of the human soul and its transcendental transformation to full expression as it moves along the creative trajectory of the earthly phase of creation and beyond, depends on the Spirit of Christ. It is the life and the fertilizer of the human soul. It is a free gift of the Spirit of His Father to mankind through Christ for the fulfillment of that one purpose of the Father for all mankind: creation

> *Come, ye blessed of my Father; inherit the kingdom prepared for you*
> *from the foundation of the world.*

> ---Matthew 25: 34

This invitation is for everyone as was portrayed in the parables of the Vineyard. The workers received equal payment of penny a day. (Matthew 20: 1-16) What those workers received in the end, metaphorically represented that one gift from the Father to all mankind: His Spirit through Christ. The parable additionally revealed that the gift is offered to us at all stages in our earthly life cycle. Some received it when they were children as was portrayed in the event when the apostles tried to stop the children from getting to Christ.

> *But Jesus called them unto him, and said, suffer little children to*
> *come unto me, and forbid them not: for of such is the kingdom of*
> *God. Verily I say unto you, whosoever shall not receive the kingdom*
> *of God as a little child shall in no wise enter therein.*

> ---Luke 18: 6-7

The ordained apostles and Paul received their own as adults. The thief crucified on Jesus's right hand got that gift few hours before his death. Paul received His own on his way to Damascus. The reward was the same for all of them. Sometimes one may have to be prepared and be patient as was portrayed in the parables of the ten virgins (Matthew 25: 1-13), and the importunate widow. (Luke 18: 1-8) The ubiquities manner on how this gift is obtained is portrayed in the parables of the hidden treasure in the field found by a farmer and the pearl of great price found by the merchant, who sold everything and bought it. (Matthew 13: 44-46) From the time of Christ to the present day, millions of people have received this gift and participated in the global banquet without realizing it. I do not know when Late President Nelson Mandela of South Africa received his own but it manifested in such a grandiose manner that the entire world witnessed it. Recent event showed that the German Chancellor, Angela Merkel, received that gift as I will portray later in this treatise. You can add to the list. Heaven and earth may pass away but this blessing through Christ, will not pass away. Inside that blessing, one can have in insight an all that Jesus revealed about human life, Himself and His Father-His love and mercy to the just and unjust.

Jesus's Kingdom of God-His Spirit in human souls- is the wine of His Christianity that He introduced to the world. This wine is not the wine offered by the priest during the Eucharist (Holy Communion). To have a taste of Jesus's Kingdom of God is to have His Spirit in our souls. Jesus knew the intrinsic value of His Spirit in human souls and invited everyone-the rich, the poor, the outcast, the homeless the blind, the refugees, the Native Americans, the Afro-Americans, the whites and the blacks in every nation and people of other religions- to have His Spirit. The Spirit of Christ is the core element in the multiple phases of human creation. We can go on killing one another in the name of the Father or another God. We can inherit this gift from Christ and join others on the evolutionary creative pathway to our glory and in making life on this planet pleasant and free of human atrocities. The gift is free. In the parable of the Sower, Jesus represented the Sower, who took the seeds- the Spirit of His Father- and scattered it to all human souls. There are no preset conditions for receiving the gift. The belief in the Father or in Jesus Christ is not a precondition for receiving that gift. It is a condition for retaining the gift as to put it to use. Belief in Christ is not a precondition for receiving the gift. Paul had no faith when he received it on his way to Damascus. However, to retain the gift and make use of it, you have to have faith in Christ and His Father.

I am the vine, ye are the branches: He that abides in me, and I in him, the same bringeth forth much fruit: for without me ye can do nothing. If a man abides not in me, he is cast forth as a branch, and is withered; and men gather them, and cast them into the fire, and they are burned.

---John 15: 5-6

The possession of His Spirit was so important to Christ and His Father, that the greatest show on earth was designed to show mankind-not just talk or show it by prophetic dreams and visions-the infinite value of the Spirit of Christ in human creation by His death and resurrection. It was a masterpiece design that was executed with precision. It opened the portals of the spiritual galaxy, that for the first time, mankind had a glimpse into their own spiritual imagery.

The big question is not how to get that gift. You do not have to do anything to be worthy of it. We are all worthy of it as proclaimed by Christ and revealed in many of His parables. The real question is now that you know you were invited to the banquet, you had a taste of Jesus's Kingdom of God-the seed was implanted into your soul-how would you hold on to it, develop it to its intended use as planned by the Father and Jesus Christ? As portrayed in the parable of the Sower, which category would you fall into as explained by Christ?

When any one hearth the word of the kingdom, and understandeth it not, then cometh the wicked one, and catcheth away that which was sown in his heart. This is he which received seed by the way side. But he that received the seed into stony places, the same is he that heareth the word, and anon with joy receiveth it; Yet hath he not root in himself, but dureth for a while: for when tribulation or persecution ariseth because of the word, by and by he is offended. He also that received seed among the thorns is he that heareth the word; and the care of this world, and the deceitfulness of riches, choke the word, and he becometh unfruitful. But he that received seed into the good ground is he that heareth the word, and understandeth it; which also beareth fruit, and bringeth forth, some an hundredfold, some sixty, some thirty.

---Matthew 13: 3-23

Are you ready for the tribulations and sacrifices associated with the attempts in this materialistic world to develop that kingdom of God within you and allow the Father and Christ to continue doing what they have been doing for mankind from the beginning of the world? There is only one will of the Father for mankind: to believe in Him and in Jesus Christ whom He sent with power and full authority to initiate and demonstrate to mankind what He learned from Him: to give His Spirit to human souls and demonstrate the earthly phase of human creation to its full spiritual expression using Himself as an example. Perhaps, we missed it because the vital information on what was revealed to the apostles, Paul and early Christians was not handed down to us. We grow up as Christians without the real knowledge why Jesus came to the world. We have to eliminate all the false conceptions of Jesus's Kingdom of God and remove the veils that obstruct our views of the narrow path so that we can see everything. Our duty was set up as to enable us participate in the earthly phase of our creation. We must keep our souls fit-by eliminating the quest for earthly power and treasures, exploitation of the poor nations, and jealousy, hatred, greed, and injustice-for the Kingdom of God, harvest its power and manifest it just like Jesus did. This open invitation for Jesus's Kingdom of God is the will of His Father, our God that we will not, even as of today, taste death, till we see its manifestations in our daily life activities as we journey to our glory. The manifestations of Jesus's Kingdom of God in our daily lives is what makes one a Christian and will be discussed later

There are laws that must be obeyed for humans to develop and manifest the spiritual powers of this Kingdom within. Are you willing, as suggested by the apostle Peter to "rid yourself of all malice, all deceit, hypocrisy, envy, slander of every kind. And like newborn babies crave pure spiritual milk, so that you may grow up in your salvation, that you have tasted that the Lord is good and real." (1 Peter 2: 1–3) The attainment of the highest spiritual evolution with the transformation of the earthly life into expressive spiritual life is the goal of Jesus's Kingdom of God that came. "Seek you first the Kingdom of God and His righteousness and all these things shall be added unto you." (Matt 6:33) We must use that vital knowledge to make the right choices: compassion for others, justice, charity, hope, optimism, reconciliation instead of anger, and avoidance of false glory, murder, rape, war, betrayal and use a brute force to settle conflicts.

And this Gospel of the Kingdom shall be preached in the entire world for a witness unto all nations, and then shall the end come.

--- Matt 24:14.

And they went forth, and preached everywhere, the Lord working with them, and confirming the word with signs following. Amen.

---Mark 16:20

Parables that depicted Rejection of Jesus's open invitation

The parable of the dishonest steward. (Luke 16:1-12)
Parable of the old and new wine. (Luke 5:36-39
The parable of the ten virgins. (Matthew 25:1-13)

The parables of the wedding feast and the unwilling guests. (Matthew 22:1-10; Luke 14:16-24)
Parable of the two sons. (Matthew 21:28-32)
The faithful and the wicked steward. ((Matthew 24:45-51; Luke 12:42-46)
The parable of the Sower. (Mark 4:3-9; Matthew 13:3-9; Luke 8:5-8)
The unforgiving servant. (Matthew 18:23-35)
The wicked husbandmen. (Matthew 22:33-44; Mark 12:1-12; Luke 20:9-19)
The sheep and the goats. (Matthew 25:31-36)
The children in the marketplace. (Matthew 11:16-19; Luke 7: 31-35)

The critical question is this: Are we also going to reject Jesus's invitation, or are we going to that wedding feast, to have the taste of the new wine: Jesus's Kingdom of God? The consequences of refusal to drink the new wine are grave and portrayed in the following parables by Christ:

The parable of the fishing net. (Matthew 13:47-50)
The tree and its fruits. (Matthew 7:15-20; Luke 6:43-49)

What Christians and their leaders must do to ward off the consequences of refusing to drink the new wine that is not mixed with the old wine is portrayed in the parable of the barren fig tree.

A certain man had a fig tree planted in his vineyard; and he came and sought fruit thereon, and found none. Then said he unto the dresser of his vineyard, Behold, these three years I come seeking fruit on this fig tree, and find none: cut it down; why cumbereth it the ground? And he answering said unto him, Lord, let it alone this

year also, till I shall dig about it, and dung it: And if it bear fruit,
well: and if not, then after that thou shalt cut it down."

---Luke 13:6-9

The Christianity as prescribed, proclaimed and practiced today will surely perish. I do not know what type of Christianity would replace it. The hand writing is on the wall. To control the downfall and avert the impending catastrophe, today's Christianity must "dig about" the seed implanted in human hearts by Christ and "dung it" by fertilizing it with what Christ prescribed, proclaimed and demonstrated in His new Christianity. This is the will of the Father. This is the will of Christ. This is our responsibility to all mankind , to oneself and to our children as prescribed by Christ. It is an irrevocable responsibility from which the Father and Jesus Christ would not release us.

CHAPTER 8

HIDDEN SECRETS OF THE KINGDOM OF GOD IN THE LORD'S PRAYER

Our Father which art in heaven, Hallowed be thy name,
Thy kingdom come; thy will be done, in earth as it is in
heaven. Give us our daily bread. And forgive us our debts
as we forgive our debtors. And lead us not into tempta-
tion, but deliver us from evil; for thine is the kingdom,
and the power, and the glory, forever. Amen.

—Matthew 6:9-13, Luke 11:2-4

God is a Spirit and those that worship Him must worship
Him in spirit and in truth.

—Jesus. John 4:24

The hidden secrets are in the following words in the Lord's Prayer:

Let thy Kingdom come
Let Thy will be done on earth and in Heaven
Give us this day our daily bread

The central beam of the iridescent heavenly light from Jesus's Kingdom of God, like the eye of the hurricane, was focused on the Lord's Prayer. That angelic prayer is the nucleus of the Kingdom of God that came. It carries with it both the holy imageries of the Father and Christ, who gave us the prayer. Additionally, it revealed the divine elements that are required for the staged earthly phase of the human creative process and for human-to-human manifestations of the divine interaction of what is being created. The first part of the prayer: our Father, who art in heaven, hallowed be thy name, let thy Kingdom come, let thy will be done on earth as in heaven, give us our daily bread, are the presumptive prologs of divine elements. The second part of the prayer: forgive us our trespasses as we forgive those that trespass against us; lead us not into temptation, but deliver us from evil, are the earthly components of the prayer, that are still tagged with some deep divine connotations. In this exposition, I will deal only with the first part of the prayer with emphases on what Jesus incorporated-His Kingdom of God-in the model prayer about Himself and the human souls, without anyone-even the apostles-realizing it.

The Lord's Prayer supersedes all other prayers because of what Jesus incorporated as core elements in that prayer: His Father, Himself and all of us. In it one finds the gift of the Kingdom of God that came for the earthly human life and for the eternal life. The goal for human life is surmised in that prayer. The essential duty of humans toward God and humanity was revealed in a nutshell in that prayer. God was revealed and His glory and design for all humans, and the essential elements for our existence and spiritual evolution were spiritually crafted in that grand Prayer. How shall we thank Jesus for that prayer? Shall we cook the best meal and invite Him to dine with us? The answer is no. Shall we then sing glories and alleluias in all our cathedrals and churches immortalizing this gift? Jesus told the young rich ruler to sell everything, and distribute to the poor. Shall we then sell everything we have and give to the poor? It is possible that Jesus does not want us to thank Him. So I have to rephrase my question. How shall we please Him and put a smile on His face? Shall we broadcast to the world that we have put our complete trust in Him, that we believe in Him and just walk away? The answer is no. To please Jesus, we must follow Him to the end of His mission-even if you have sold everything and given to the poor- to learn from Him how to love His Father and your fellow humans as was written: "You shall love the Lord your God with all your heart and with all your soul and with all your mind." And the second is like it. "You shall love your neighbor as yourself" Additionally-and this is equally as important as the above two great commandments- we must learn how to open our hearts to Jesus's Kingdom of God. After we have done all the things that I have suggested above, Jesus could still say to us that we are still ignorant of why He came down to our planet; that we have failed to comprehend the best of all His miracles, staged in three acts over the time period He was with us.

1. Let thy Kingdom come

But seek ye first the kingdom of God, and his righteousness; and all these shall be added unto you.

---Matthew 6:33

Ask, and it (His Kingdom) shall be given you, seek, and ye shall find, knock, and it shall be opened unto you.

---Luke 11:9

The Lord's Prayer is the best divine instructions given to humans for the development and manifestation of Jesus's Kingdom of God. It revealed some of the mysteries of the Kingdom of God that we were instructed to petition for its coming. One has to have a good understanding of what is this Kingdom of God as to appreciate the instruction given in the Lord's Prayer. The petition for His Kingdom to come is a request for the Father to give us the Spirit of Christ-His Spirit through Christ-and the courage to manifest it. Jesus Kingdom of God was not something that descended from heaven in a day or something we must pray for as to come in future. The way it comes was portrayed in the parable of the generous employer who paid his workers equally although they were employed at different times of the day. (Matthew 20:1-16) They were all given the same gift from His Father: the Kingdom of God. The apostles were the first to receive it. A Nigerian proverb states the whenever a person wakes up is the start of his or her day. The petition for the Kingdom to come portrays your readiness to have it immediately-to have a taste of Jesus's Kingdom of God. We have to follow Jesus to Golgotha and beyond to see how to obtain it, develop and manifest what Christ prescribed, proclaimed and demonstrated on this Kingdom. You will then understand why the Master of Wisdom added for us to petition for the Kingdom of God to come.

The Kingdom of God we were instructed to pray to come is not for a new spiritual universe or a spiritual earth where His Father reigns. It is not for a new Kingdom on earth designed to have the same divine features as the spiritual Kingdom where God resides. It is not Paradise regained or the New Earth and the New Jerusalem that came down from heaven as was recorded in the book of Revelation. It is a petition for our entry into the paradise of the human soul-Jesus's Kingdom of God-now. That one promise of the Father is to give us the Kingdom-His Spirit through Christ. That was what the Father had promised us and "the Father knows what we have need of before we ask Him." (Matthew 6:8). However, the Father wants to hear it from us. Are we ready for it? Jesus's Kingdom of God would help us develop an impeccable, non-illusionary divine essence-that is required as core elements in our souls for what the Father is creating through Jesus Christ.

The epistemology of how Jesus develops this creative power with the human souls is beyond human comprehension. As I searched the Gospel for the weaponry one has to use as to harvest the fruits of the divine union with the Spirit of Christ, it became obvious that the best weaponry was found in the Lord's Prayer. Its introduction was the most important instructions ever given to humans for our spiritual evolution.

The human experience of Jesus's Kingdom of God reveals the human potentials of what the Father is creating. Let us pray to the Father therefore for Jesus's Kingdom of God to come to us even as we sleep! Abba Father, give us Jesus's Spirit! Let the Spirit you gave to Jesus come to us through Him. Let that spirit of Christ who gave us this prayer, spiritualize our souls that we may proceed to attain full expression of Jesus's divine image. Let your experience of Jesus's Kingdom-the divine union of His Spirit with your soul-be the spiritual weaponry you must use to trust in God, His Father. Let the divine bondage of our souls with the Father and with Jesus be the weaponry the rich and the poor, the just and the unjust, those we love and our enemies, people of other faith, must use to demonstrate to Jesus that it is easier for all of us, not just the rich, to enter this Kingdom than a camel to go through the eye of a needle. The triumph of the immortal human spirit, the glory and the diadem of our souls, the ultimate human joy and destiny is our association with Jesus's Kingdom of God. Let every heart prepare a room for this Kingdom of the Spirit of Christ for surely the Father will not withdraw His only promise to His children-the gift of His Spirit through Christ. That promise was the Kingdom that came to be used for our creation: the production of the spiritual mankind.

We must strive together towards one goal: divine consolidation of God-Jesus-human unity and experience in prayer and action. To pray to God esoterically means your acceptance of the existence of God and His omnipresence. It invokes an infinite association of God with you and you with God who is near you and hears you. We were told by Jesus that before you open your mouth that God already knows what is in your heart. To ask the Father for the Kingdom of God to come, esoterically is to ask for the Spirit of Christ to come to you.

God is a Spirit and they that worship Him must worship Him in spirit and in truth.

---John, 4:24

We must worship the Father in spirit. Perhaps, to worship or pray to Him means that you must worship Him in spirit and allow your inherited human spirit to move out of the bones and flesh at the moment of that association. If you are not able to translate or transfigure to that metaphysical state when you pray to God, then it is possible that you may not be praying at all. It is the human spirit that prays. It is for this reason that Jesus suggested that when you pray, that you should go to your inner room and close all doors. "When you pray, enter into thy closet, and when thou hast shut up door, pray to thy Father who sees in secret shall reward thee openly." (Matt. 6:6) When you pray to the Father, you may be praying in the presence of other invisible audience, of which Jesus, His twelve apostles, the angels, other great prophets and wise men may be present. We believe in the omnipresence of God. But that omnipresence also translates to Jesus, and all the angels, even to the Devil and his demons. They are all watching us at all times, especially when we pray. The spiritual audience waits to hear your prayer. The degree of the purity of your heart determines the extent and the composition of the spiritual audience. When your heart is very pure, the audience is large, composed of the Father, Jesus and His twelve holy men and hosts of angels. The Devil and his demons would not be present. God who is "a discerner of thoughts and intents of the heart" knows what is in the hearts of all people at all times. When your heart is not pure, and God knows you have not come for a change of heart, neither the Father nor the angelic audience would be there to hear your prayer. The only audience one gets is the Devil and his demon.

The transfiguration of Jesus in the presence of Peter, James and John, was one of the occasions in which Jesus stepped out of the flesh and bones, regained temporarily His glory and was able to communicate with the spirits of Moses and Elias, if the appearances of Moses and Elias is true. Jesus frequently left His audience and went to isolated places to pray. It is within the realm of possibility that on those occasions His Spirit stepped out of the flesh temporarily to enable Him to communicate with the Father. He did not want anybody to witness those mini-transfigurations. The disciple Stephen, 'a wise man full of faith and the Holy Ghost', as reported in the Acts of the Apostles manifested these phenomena of human transfiguration when the Jews brought him before the council and accused him of blasphemous words against Moses and against their God.

When Stephen addressed the council in Jerusalem, "all that sat in the council, looking steadfastly on him, saw his face as it had been the face of an angel." Act 6:15. And subsequently as he was being stoned, "being full of the Holy Ghost, looked up steadfastly into heaven, and saw the glory of God, and Jesus standing on the right hand of God" Act 7:55. At the moment of the above encounter, the spiritual body of Stephen had stepped out of the flesh and what the audience saw like the face of an angel was indeed the face of the spiritual body of Stephen. Peter, James and John reported that the face of the transfigured Jesus " did shine as the sun and His raiment was as the light" Jesus at that time appeared to be talking to Moses and Elias, just as Stephen petitioned to the Lord Jesus, to receive his spirit and forgive the people who were stoning him. At Pentecost, with the gift of the Holy Ghost, the spiritual bodies of the apostles translated, that they were able to speak in tongues, the original language of all spirits, that the spirits of those who were present could understand them. To associate with God, Jesus or any of the great prophets that had departed from world, to communicate with members of the invisible world, the human spirit must also transfigure and revert to a spiritual status. Jesus did not take Peter, James and John to a mountain to be transfigured for a show. Nay, it was a demonstration on how we could communicate and associate with the unseen spiritual world. Prayer is one of the *modus operandi* for penetrating into the metaphysical world. The Spirit of Jesus Christ prepares us on how to participate in such endeavors. The accomplishment of the spiritual transformation means that the Kingdom of God has indeed come unto you with power.

Prayer brings out the power of that Kingdom of God within you. Jesus said: "There are many standing here that will not taste death until they see the Kingdom of God come with power." It manifests as a result of power of Christ in you. Many have questioned the value of prayer at all; stating that many prayers have failed to protect us against evil or help us secure a job or recover from an illness. Many prayers are unanswered because of our inability to penetrate into the spiritual realm of God, Jesus and the angels. It is the result of our inability to utilize the Kingdom of God within us. For many years we sought earthly treasures, refused to sell anything and give to the poor, transformed mankind into killing machines and grossly neglected the most important promise of the Father: Jesus's Kingdom of God. How can they hear our prayers when we have neglected to teach our children the nature of the Good News that Jesus introduced to the world. How can they hear our prayers when mankind has been destroying what the Father was creating and have put in place equipment to stall that process? How can they answer our prayers when the knowledge, so vital for the Father and Jesus Christ to continue creating humans is distorted, and hidden for the last two thousand years. How can they answer our prayer when many false Gospel of the Kingdom replaced the true Gospel of Jesus's Kingdom of God? How can they hear our prayers when we have deliberately trashed and rejected Jesus's Kingdom of God? In fact, we deliberately cut the thread that connects us to His Father. However, do not be discouraged; keep praying for "it is your Father's Good pleasure to give you the Kingdom." (Luke 12:32) For "if you, being evil-lack the basic understanding of the Kingdom of God that came-know how to give good gifts unto your children; how much more shall your heavenly Father give the Holy Spirit-the Spirit of Christ-to them that ask Him." (Luke 11:13) This promise of the Father cannot be broken if we continue to pray for Jesus's Kingdom-the Spirit that He got from the Father-to come.

Sometimes, when we pray, we are worried about the current economic conditions, the jobless state of the economy, the oil, gas, gold, and diamond markets, our pension and retirement. We are angry at those that abused and lied to us; we have pledged to take revenge. All these activities prevent our creating a spiritual environment, and prevent our gaining temporal entrance to God's presence when we pray. But for the few who have gained knowledge of Jesus's Kingdom of God, and have developed His spiritual powers and are poor in spirit, their prayers are answered. They "live in spirit and walk in spirit." and pray in spirit. They bear the burden of others. They do not wish for anything materialistic and yet they lack nothing. They pray not just for themselves or their families, but they also pray for the world and for all humanity. They believe in one true God, introduced to the world by Jesus Christ, as the Father and creator of all and control the common destiny for all humans. They do not pray for power to perform miracles. They manifest themselves Jesus's miracles. They do not ask for money to pray for others. Although Jesus gave the instruction for us to pray to God directly, they still pray to God through Jesus. The truth is that the tools one can use to translate or transfigure and step out of yourself when you pray, is in this very prayer. I will refer to them as the preparatory ingredients for creating a spiritual environment for successful spiritual communication with Jesus and His Father or any of the holy angels when you pray. You have to go through that ritual or you have not prayed at all.

Let thy will be done on earth as it is done in heaven

I came down from heaven, not to do mine own will but the will of Him that sent me.

---John 6:38

And this is the will of Him that sent me that every one which seeth the Son, and believeth on him, may have everlasting life; and I will raise him up at the last day."

---John 6:39

Verily, verily, I say unto you, He that heareth my word, and believe in Him that sent me, hath everlasting life, and shall not come into condemnation; but is passed from death unto life.

---John 5:24

And this is the will of the Father which hath sent me, that of all which He hath given me, I should lose nothing, but shall raise it up at the last day.

---Jesus

There is only one will of the Father for mankind. This prayer reveals to us what the will of God is. That will for mankind is this: to believe in Jesus Christ and obey His commandments. We do not know how it is done in heaven. The apostles did not ask how the will of God is done in heaven. If how that will is done in heaven is revealed today, it will not only make Headline News as the 'Breaking News', but there will be complete analysis of it on the 'Situation Room' of CNN by panels of experts. If we are to honor God, if we are to drink that living water that leads to everlasting life, then we must do the will of God to be called the children of God, and the brothers and sisters of Jesus by entering into Jesus's Kingdom of God. This Kingdom of God is at the door of every entrance that leads to His Father. Inside the capsule of that Kingdom of God is the robe of Jesus's new Christianity and what Christ prescribed as our task in complying with the will of God

For whosoever shall do the will of God, the same is my brother, and my sister and mother.

---Mark 3:35.

How do we know the will of this God who prepared a Kingdom from the beginning for us that we may come and inherit it? How do we know the will of God who through Jesus gave us instruction that we may love Him with all our hearts and soul and love one another? How do we know the will of God whose Kingdom and whose righteousness we must seek? How do we know the will of this God who has numbered our very hairs on our head (means He know of where about of all humans)? How do we know the will of God who watches over sparrows feeds birds of the air, clothes the lilies of the field, makes His sun to rise on the good and on the evil and send rain on the just and unjust? The answer is in the Lord's Prayer. Most of the atrocities and evil committed here on earth were done because the people that committed those offenses believed they were fulfilling the will of God. The greatest tragedy in the history of humanity is "the blind guides leading the blind," (Luke 6:39) and those that "sit on Moses' seat" giving guidance and interpreting the will of God. (Matthew 23:16)

Jesus of Nazareth, revealed in His own person, exemplary activities that demonstrated the will of God as was also portrayed in this angelic Prayer. He finished the work that God gave Him to do. For the accomplishment of that work, we have to follow Jesus to Golgotha to see how it was accomplished. The will of God for you may not be the same as for Jesus of Nazareth. The will of God for us is simple: believe in Jesus Christ, accept his invitation to drink the new wine and inherit His Kingdom of God. This is the will of God. This is the whole duty of man. The spiritual weaponry for the accomplishment of this was crafted in Jesus' Gospel and made manifest by the spiritual Cross is what the Lord's Prayer is all about. Jesus's Kingdom of God puts those who enter into it on the trajectory of the earthly evolutionary phase of human creation that leads to full expression of who we are.

I am the light of the world. Whosoever follows me will never walk in darkness, but will have the light of life.

---John 8:12.

Follow that light from Jesus's kingdom of God. It will reveal its mysteries to you that you too like Paul may know the spiritual weaponry in the Gospel crafted for your eternal life. The synopsis of it is the Lord's Prayer. Although my knowledge of the spiritual weaponry for execution of the will of God is incomplete, however, I do know that acquisition of blood diamond, blood oil, unjustified wars that drive people from their homes to refugee camps, cheating, false documentations of economic data for personal gain, racism, claims for super nationalism, illegal arms deals, superior religion or super individualism are not the will of God and are not found in the bag of tools for eternal life or in this Lord's prayer. The Lord's Prayer provided the weaponry for the realization and expression of the will of God that was proclaimed as a constant reminder of our duty for the restoration of God – human habitation. This is the only purpose in life. All other purposes are of lower order. As finites, we do not know all the essentials and absolute perfections of God's nature and His righteousness. But we do know, as narrated to us by eye witnesses, the manner of Jesus' life and His perfect obedience to the will of His Father. The events at Golgotha revealed many important aspects of that will of God.

Give us this day, our daily bread

> *Labor not for the meat which perisheth, but for that which endureth unto everlasting life, which the Son of man shall give unto you.*

> *---John 6:27*

> *I am the bread of life; he that cometh to me shall never hunger; and he that believeth in me shall never thirst.*

> *---John 6:35*

This bread is not the food we eat. This bread is not the food you eat every day, neither is it what you drink to quest your thirst. Jesus said to the disciples, "Do you not understand that whatsoever enters in at the mouth goes to the belly and is cast out in the draught." (Matthew 15:17) Why must He tell you to pray for food to eat? The heavenly Father knows you need food, made provision for you to have it even before you ask. Jesus said; "seek not what you shall eat, or what you shall drink, neither be ye of doubtful mind. For all these things do the nations of the world seek after; and your Father knows that you have need of these things. But seek ye the Kingdom of God; and all these things shall be added unto you. Fear not little flock; for it is your Father's good pleasure to give you the Kingdom." (Luke: 12:29-32) The divine instruction is for us to pray for the true bread from heaven. The bread is the metaphoric expression for the Spirit of Christ.

> *Man does not live on bread alone, but on every word that comes from the mouth of God.*

> ---Matthew 4:4.

Jesus addressed Himself as the bread of Life "I am the bread of Life." To ask God to give us this bread daily is the petition to the Father for the Spirit of Jesus to come into our hearts, that we may have experience of the Kingdom of God within us that came.

> *This is the bread that comes down from heaven, so that one may eat of it and not die.... Whoever eats this bread will live forever.*

> ---Jesus.

To eat this bread is to enter into Jesus's Kingdom of God and put on the robe of the new Christianity as prescribed, proclaimed and demonstrated by Christ. Many that will truly eat this bread daily from the Father, to them will be given the power of the Kingdom of God that came. To ask God to give us our daily bread shows deeply your love and strong desire to be fully created as showcased by Jesus on the day of His resurrection. The Lord's Prayer is a model divine instruction for eternal life. Let this Kingdom of Christ come-this is the promise of the Father to mankind. Let the glori-fied Spirit of Jesus interact with your soul and help you to manifest this Kingdom. Take the bread of life every day. In essence, let the Spirit of Jesus Christ into your heart-to regenerate and transform your soul to the spiritual fire of transfiguration in your journey to eternal life that will enable you gain access to the spiritual world of His Father.

And all things whatsoever ye shall ask in prayer believing, ye shall receive.

---Jesus. Matthew 21:22.

CHAPTER 9

FUTURE KINGDOM OF GOD REDISCOVERED

The only way one can get a handle on the meaning of Jesus's future Kingdom of God is to know in the first place what the kingdom of God that Jesus proclaimed is. It is also necessary to remove from your consciousness all the Old Testament texts, used by the Christian theologians and religious leaders to reveal the nature of that Kingdom. Many theologians, supported by the Christian leaders, have used the Old Testament literature to indicate that Jesus's future kingdom of God will be a spiritual kingdom on Earth patterned after the Jewish apocalyptic vision of the Prophets-Daniel, Ezekiel and Hosea. The eschatologists had again looked at the Old Testament literature and projected their findings to Jesus's future Kingdom of God. Albert Schweitzer, in his book: *The mystery of the Kingdom of God: the Secret of Jesus's Messiahship and Passion* portrayed Jesus's Kingdom of God as an ethical and as an eschatological fact. Jesus's future Kingdom of God was again clothed with the prophetic visions of the expectations of the Jewish people. It was relegated to the time when the God of Moses, through the expected Messiah, would save Israel and restore the promised earthly spiritual Kingdom to Israel.

The inability to understand the kingdom of God that Jesus proclaimed, led the Church leaders and the theologians to look at the Old Testament literatures for answers on Jesus's future kingdom of God. To seek any type of explanation for the Old Testament texts is like seeking the living from among the dead. Jesus's kingdom of God, whether conceived in the past, present or the future, was completely a new paradigm that was introduced to the world. To seek the understanding of future Kingdom of God through the Jewish prophetic utterances, and the apocalyptic Gospel texts, is to sail an uncharted sea. As referenced by Jesus, it is like "a thief and a robber, who entered into the sheepfold, not by the door, but climbed up some other way. But the sheep will not follow him: they flee from him: for they know not the voice of strangers." (John 10: 1, 5)

Jesus did not come to establish a kingdom on earth where His Father will reign forever. When He was arrested by the Jews, He made a public proclamation that "My kingdom is not of this world." Jesus refused to set a time limit for the Kingdom that He proclaimed. The growth and the evolutionary nature of that kingdom suggest that it will end when earthly human life ends. What Jesus did with His Spirit-the Spirit of the Father in Him-for mankind, before His death and resurrection and what He did for everyone after His death and resurrection with his glorified risen Spirit-the holy Spirit-are not two separate events. They are of the same continuous, irrevocable activities in human creation that are still going on today. The final act of that metaphysical drama is not the revelation that Jesus is the Messiah or the creation of the apocalyptic new heaven and earth as envisioned by the Jewish prophets. The transcendental drama catapulted the incarnated human souls with the Spirit of Christ to a new mode of existence-a new creature in a spiritual world of Christ and His Father. It is an eternal drama, publically demonstrated by Christ that reveals everything you want to know about Jesus's Kingdom of God-the past, the present and the future. They are all linked with the same thread- the Spirit of Christ and for the same purpose: creation of the spiritual mankind.

Jesus proclaimed an active Kingdom that came and is within us-His Spirit in human souls. There is no gulf between its present and the future. There was a quiescent period of fifty days for His ascension and the day of Pentecost when His risen Spirit-the Holy Ghost-resumed its earthly activities. Since then, even as of today there are what would seem to be quiescent periods in the activities of Jesus's Kingdom of God. However, there are no resting periods. As long as human beings are on this planet, Jesus's Kingdom of God lives and will continue to be with us to eternity. Jesus did not reveal any eschatological or apocalyptic nature of that Kingdom. Jesus's Kingdom of God was the gift from His Father that came already as promised. I have, throughout this treatise revealed what Jesus did for us with that gift from His Father. However, Jesus had to depart from this planet Earth. The earthly phase of human creation must continue. How then can His kingdom of God continue without His Spirit? Jesus promised that He would come back. Jesus told His apostles "for verily I say unto you, ye shall not have gone over the cities of Israel, till the Son of man be come." (Matthew 10: 23) The Christians are still waiting for Him to come back. However, Jesus already came back, not in human form or like the risen Christ that was seen on the day of His resurrection. The glorified Spirit of the risen Christ came back on the day of Pentecost as the Holy Ghost.

*But the Comforter, which is the Holy Ghost, whom the Father will send **in my name**, he shall teach you all things, and bring to your remembrance, whatsoever I have said unto you.*

---John 14:26

Timing was very important in the execution of the Father's business. The crucifixion of Jesus was carried out during the week of the Passover feast. The Father and Jesus Christ wanted the people who came to Jerusalem from many parts of the world to witness that event. The promised gift from heaven must also be given at a time when people from many parts of the world would come again to Jerusalem for an occasion to witness the glorious event. The Father and His Son waited until the time was fulfilled. The Pentecost feast, a festival of thanks for the harvest, and remembered as the time when the Law was given to the Israelites on Sinai was celebrated on the fiftieth day from the Passover feast. Jesus had told His apostles not to leave Jerusalem.

> *And when the day of the Pentecost was fully come, they (the apostles) were all with one accord in one place. And suddenly there came a sound from heaven as of a rushing mighty wind, and it filled the entire house where they were sitting. And there appeared unto them cloven tongues like as of fire, and it filled the entire house where they were sitting. And there appeared unto them cloven tongues like as of fire, and it sat upon each of them. And they were filled with the Holy Ghost, and began to speak with other tongues, as the Spirit gave them utterance.* Acts 2:1-4

That event was a demonstration of permanent spiritualization of the souls of the apostles. Jesus referred to this 'cloven tongues like as of fire' that sat upon the heads of the apostles on the day of the Pentecost as the wind. "The wind bloweth where it listed, and thou hearest the sound thereof, but cannot tell whence it cometh, and wither it goeth; so is every one that is born of the Spirit." (John 3:8) The wind is the glorified spirit of risen Christ, also referred to as the Spirit of the truth: "Even the Spirit of truth; whom the world cannot receive, because it seeth Him not, neither knoweth Him;

but ye knoweth him; for He dwelleth with you and shall be in you." (John 14:17) That glorified Spirit of Christ would be in all the human souls as we embark on our creative journey for full expression of our spiritual nature. The power of Christ-human soul co-union-Jesus's Kingdom of God-was exhibited on the day of Pentecost. "Verily I say unto you, that there be some of them that stand here, which shall not taste death, till they have seen the kingdom of God come with power." (Mark 9:1) On that day His Kingdom of God came again with full power!

The apostles did not know where the power that sat upon them came from, but they knew it came from their Master, who was crucified, died and rose from the dead. That Spirit remained in them and guided them in all they did for their Master and for humanity. The Jews and the people from other nations, who were present at Jerusalem, witnessed the manifestations of Jesus's Kingdom of God were amazed. They knew that a spectacular event had occurred. "Now when this was noised abroad, the multitude (Jews, devout men, out of every nation under heaven) came together, and was confounded, because that every man heard them speak in his own language. And they were all amazed and marveled, saying one to another, Behold, are not all these which speak Galileans? And how hear we every man in our own tongue, were in we were born?" (Acts 2:5-8) Jesus Christ and His Father, kept their promise. "But wait for the promise of the Father, which ye heard of me. For John truly baptized with water, but ye shall be baptized with the Holy Ghost not many days hence." (Acts 1:4-5)

It was a spiritual event that gives humankind direct access to the glorified Spirit of Christ. Its conception was spiritual. Its dispensation was from the Father. It opened a door for all who are able to receive that glorified Spirit of Jesus that came back on the day of Pentecost, to enter into the staged the trajectory of the evolutionary creative process that was hidden from wise men and the

Prophets. It manifested as Jesus's Kingdom of God in the lives of all who received it. Many who truly received that Spirit have manifested the glory and the blessings of Jesus's Kingdom of God. Paul, in the presence of witnesses, received the Spirit of the risen Christ on his way to Damascus.

There is no transcendental gulf between Jesus's Kingdom of God that came before His death and resurrection and His Kingdom that came to the apostles, Paul and others, after His ascension. The 'present' and 'future' Jesus's kingdom of God referred to time sequence of events and not to any prophetic visions of a Kingdom that would be 'consummated' when He returns. The Spirit of Christ in human souls-His kingdom of God-before His death was that the same Jesus's Kingdom of God that came after His ascension-the Spirit of the glorified risen Christ that the Father sent in the name of Christ. The Holy Ghost when viewed as a separate Spirit, seem as an isolated Spirit that contributed nothing to what Jesus accomplished. The Father sent down the glorified Holy Spirit of the risen Christ as the Comforter (the Holy Ghost). Any interpretation of Jesus's Kingdom of God that came and is within us would be meaningless if we are dealing with two different spiritual entities spiritualizing human souls with the Spirit of the Father. There is a continuous trend between Jesus's Kingdom of God that came before His death and the one that came to the apostles on the day of Pentecost and to Paul on his way to Damascus. All power and authority was given to Jesus by His Father for this Kingdom of God and not to another Spirit. Putting it all together, the Holy Ghost is the Spirit of the risen Christ.

Many Christians are waiting for Jesus Christ to come back again. Many are still waiting for Jesus's future Kingdom of God to be consummated. Jesus Christ is not sitting on the right hand of God waiting for us to come unto Him, be showered with the gift of His Spirit and receive everlasting life. Then at the appointed time-envisioned by the Christians as Advent or the period of Rapture-to return give everlasting life to the 'faithful, defeat the Satan and restore His kingdom on earth. This concept is one of the greatest obstacle to the understanding Jesus's task from His Father and the evolution of His Spirit in human souls. Jesus's Kingdom of God is a continuous transcendental process that is still going on even as of today. Its future depends on your activating that Kingdom within you. It will continue in future to the 'futuristic' time as appointed by the Father when human creation will stop.

> *It is not for you to know the times or the seasons, which the Father hath put in his own power. But ye shall receive power, after that the Holy Ghost is come upon you: and ye shall be witnesses unto me both in Jerusalem, and in all Judaea, and in Samaria, and unto the uttermost part of the earth.*

> ---Jesus. Acts 1:7-8

CHAPTER 10

GROWTH OF THE KINGDOM OF GOD IN PARABLES

The comprehension of the growth of Jesus's Kingdom of God depends on the knowledge of what it is, its objectives and goal. Without this knowledge, the meaning of Jesus's parables of the growth of the Kingdom would remain hidden. There are four recorded parables of the growth of the Kingdom in the Gospel. There may be more or less, as it depends on the author's definition of growth.

The seed growing secretly. Mark 4:26-29; Matthew 13:24-30
The Mustard seed. Matthew 13:31-32; Luke 13:18-19
The Leaven. Matthew 13:13; Luke 13:20-21
The Sower and the seeds. Matthew 13:3-9; Mark 4:3-9;
Luke 8:5-8

Jesus's Kingdom of God is like, "the seed which a man cast into the ground, and should sleep, and rise night and day, and the seed should spring and grow up, he knoweth not how. For the earth bringeth forth fruit of herself; first the blade, then the ear, after that the full corn in the ear. But when the fruit is brought forth, immediately he putteth in the sickle, because the harvest is come." (Mark 4:26-29" Its growth as depicted in the above parable is irrepressible. It will increase and expand worldwide, bearing with it the flagship of the human soul, decorated with the everlasting words of God-the Spirit of the Father-given to us by Jesus Christ. This Kingdom of God grows secretly to fulfill all its goals, with no interference from mankind as was portrayed in the above parable of Christ. The reason is simple: Jesus's Kingdom of God is linked to human creation. For mankind, human creation is the ultimate goal of the Kingdom of God. However, for the planted seed to grow to full corn, it must be watered not by the blood of Jesus or the blood of the martyrs, but by the knowledge of what the goals of the Kingdom of God are and our ability to activate Jesus's Kingdom of God within us. I have discussed the objectives and goals of Jesus's Kingdom of God in another epiphany, Jesus Christ, His apostles, Paul and others were murdered for what Jesus revealed on this Kingdom of God. We have to take that speck of light where they left it, put it on a "candle stick" as metaphorically suggested by Jesus, to give light to the world. Jesus proclaimed that "I am the Light." Christianity as prescribed, proclaimed and practiced today, is an obstacle to that light. At the same time there are people all over the world, who in the past tendered to the seed that was planted by watering and fertilizing it. Today, there are people doing the same. The list of people helping in the growth is inexhaustible but here are some of them:

All who seek to stop all wars and murder of human beings
All who are helping the migrant refugees of today
All who promote world peace and justice and have used tolerance and negotiations instead of war to accomplish their objectives.

All who would never take from poor nations or from the poor in their country, even though they have the opportunity and power to do so.

All who use the proceeds from their natural resources to help the poor, educate them, provide adequate health services, alleviate their sufferings, and build an enviable infrastructure for economic growth of the nation.

All who hate hypocrisy and greed, envy, worship of idols, racism, and discrimination.

All who seek the truth that Jesus revealed.

All who have developed expressions of a pure heart and worship the Father in truth.

All who have knowledge of the Father and Jesus Christ and use it to work for humanity.

All who believe in Jesus Christ and in His Father's plan for mankind.

All who love all that the Lord created and are servants to humanity and to God.

All the blessings of Jesus's Kingdom of God belong to them. Jesus belongs to them. The Father belongs to them. By the purity of their hearts, by the rejection of all that Jesus rejected, by their refusal to serve the evil and cruel men and women in power and authority-rulers of darkness-and by their obedience to the will of God, they too must rejoice, not because of what they have done for humanity, but they must rejoice because their names are written in heaven. The glory of the infinite bondage with the Father and Jesus Christ belong to them. They must rejoice because Christ has claimed their souls for this new divine Trinity of their spirits with His Father and Him.

The growth of Jesus's Kingdom of God is irrepressible for one simple reason: it is what powers, propels and sustains all the phases in human creation as a demonstration by Christ in His everlasting miracle of the earthly stages of human creation. Jesus used

Himself as the model to show what the Father and He have been doing in the past. The predictive future irrepressible growth was portrayed in the parable of mustard seed:

> *The kingdom of heaven is like to a grain of mustard seed, which a man took, and sowed in his field: Which indeed is the least of all seeds: but when it is grown, it is the greatest among herbs, and becometh a tree, so that the birds of the air come and lodge in the branches thereof.*

---Matthew 13: 31-32

Jesus's Kingdom of God is so lively and dynamic that it never sleeps. It is like brain cell and their tentacles that works days and nights even when we are asleep. It grows without Temples and Cathedrals, channeling mankind to the trajectory of the earthly phase of human creation and beyond. The story of the journey of the human soul is the story of the Spirit of Christ in human souls, moving it to an exalted transcendental evolutionary growth, manifesting along its path, love for the Father and for Christ. It prides itself for its ability to love everyone and extends that love to the enemy. It is deeply rooted in forgiveness regardless of the offense. As it moves along on its path of is growth, it garnishes every available tool for human creation and a proof for absolute trust in the Father as our God and for the obedience of His will.

> *Whosoever shall not receive the kingdom of God as a little child shall in no wise enter therein.*

---Luke 18: 7

This Kingdom of God grows like a child, thinks like a child and reacts to its entire environment like a child. A child is an interesting human being. Endowed with the highest power of physical and spiritual growth, observation, intellect, language, and skill, development in science and technology become elementary. The child is not interested in worldly possessions or power or in any form of violence. If allowed to live in his or her own world, the child would perform his or her own duty and leave the earth to be a component of the divine union. But these children are encouraged to struggle for earthly power and wealth and coached to practice hatred, discrimination, and racism. Some of them are kidnapped, abused, forced into child labors, forced to wear soldiers' uniforms to fight a war, forced to steal, and forced to live in refugee camps. To enter into Jesus's Kingdom of God, to allow the Kingdom to grow, humankind must perform like a child, think like a child, hope like a child, believe like a child, and grow up maintaining all the qualities of a child in order for the mustard seed, planted in our souls ,to grow and be the largest of all trees.

In medicine, the effective function of the blood platelets in controlling bleeding is not measured in numbers but by its effectiveness in promoting clotting process. Fifty thousand platelets can be more effective than one million platelets. A religion cannot be judged by sheer number if its members or by the number of attendance at its church services. The progression of Jesus's Kingdom of God depends on what Christ, prescribed, proclaimed and demonstrated by the epitome of His life and measured by the number of people that achieved its objectives and goals. . The growth of Jesus's Kingdom of God is measured by the number of people with "Christ in me' who along this earthly phase of creation are led by that Spirit. This was well portrayed in Jesus's parable of the Sower by "the seed that fell on good ground, and did yield fruit that sprang up and increased; and brought forth, some thirty, and some sixty, and some an hundred." (Mark 4:8)

For as many as are led by the Spirit of God, they are the sons of God.

--- Romans 8:14

Those with "Christ in me" may not even know it and may not belong to any Christian community. Those who may be boasting that they have "Christ in me" may have nothing and yet call themselves Christians. The gross misunderstanding of the evolutionary nature of Jesus's Kingdom of God made it impossible to envision what Jesus was trying to convey to His audience, the meaning of that Kingdom that he proclaimed. Jesus's introduction of a new paradigm in His Kingdom of God, with the parable of the mustard seed, even made the situation more incomprehensible. People have associated the parable of the mustard seed with the great spiritual Kingdom of God Jesus will establish on earth that will be the greatest of all Kingdoms. Jesus's Kingdom of God is not a place in heaven or on earth.

The divine union of His Kingdom of God-His Spirit-with the human souls-is not the final event. It must be activated. It must grow and mature. I have used this platform to explore the growth of Jesus's Kingdom of God in two segments-the growth of infinite union of the Spirit of Christ with the human souls and the worldwide growth in the number of human souls that received His Spirit. What is Christianity started with Jesus's Kingdom of God and ends with the infinite trinity of the human souls with the Spirit of His Father and Christ. This is the goal of Jesus's Kingdom of God. It empowers the human soul, guides it, and propels it along its creative trajectory as its objectives as to achieve its goal as was planned by the Father and demonstrated by Christ in His epic miracle of human creation. The achievement of this goal is the true measure of the growth of Jesus's Kingdom of God. Some Christian theologians have stated correctly that Christianity is an evolutionary religion. Christianity of Christ is Jesus's Kingdom of God growing secretly like a fine thread in human souls. It is this fine thread, deeply rooted in human souls, that connects us together as one common community with His Father, our God and Jesus Christ. Do not be afraid to enter into this Kingdom and let its invisible power educate and instruct you on compassion, love that extends to the enemies, peace, tolerance, forgiveness, justice, and mercy as you embark on the journey to eternal life. Be the teacher of this vital information to the people of the world by the examples of your lifestyle as prescribed and demonstrated by Christ for the growth of the Kingdom. Mankind is involved in all the words and works of Christ. My dear readers, with the knowledge of what I have so far revealed, do you think that Jesus's Kingdom of God is in you?

Fear not, little flock; for it is your Father's good pleasure to give you the kingdom. Sell that ye have, and give alms; provide yourselves bags which wax not old, a treasure in the heavens that faileth not, where no thief approacheth, neither moth corrupteth. For where your treasure is, there will your heart be also.

---Luke 12:32-34

CHAPTER 11

THE GREATEST CONSPIRACY AGAINST JESUS'S KINGDOM OF GOD.

And from the days of John the Baptist until now the kingdom of heaven suffereth violence, and the violent take it by force.

—Matthew 11:12

There are so many different interpretations of Jesus Kingdom of God that made it impossible to give a meaningful collective review on the subject. These different interpretations are not only by the Christian theologians but also by the Churches and their leaders. No one has been able to give a meaningful interpretation of Jesus's Kingdom of God. To compound the problem, although the Kingdom of God was the core message of Jesus, He refused to define what He meant by it, although He claimed that He revealed the mysteries of it to the apostles. However neither the apostles nor Paul gave any definition of Jesus's Kingdom of God. If they did, we do not know what happened to those records. It is not my intention in this epiphany to summarize the works on Jesus's Kingdom of God by the

Church and the Christian leaders. The endeavor would be an end-less effort and would not contribute to the understanding of Jesus's Kingdom of God. I do not plan to offer reflections of my work on Jesus's Kingdom of God based on their works on the subject. I have, under the bibliographies on the Kingdom of God, listed the books that I read on the Kingdom of God that Jesus proclaimed.

The style that I used in my presentation on Jesus's Kingdom of God, is first to introduce what I considered to be the new revela-tions. Then briefly explore the current concepts on the subject as to justify the explanatory platforms of the new paradigms on Jesus's Kingdom of God that I have introduced. With that information available, the reader would be able to follow-and not be confused-as the deeper revelations on the mysteries of Jesus's Kingdom of God are revealed in all the words and works of Christ. To glimpse at the light of Jesus's Kingdom of God as it powers all the events in His words and works and guide the human soul in its journey, all-with no exception-the current human doctrines and sacraments Christianity as practiced today are obstacles that have to be removed from our consciousness as to know what is that Jesus's Kingdom of God, His mission, who He is and the Father that He revealed to us.

As I explored untouched grounds in the Gospel as to under-stand the meaning of Jesus's Kingdom of God, I uncovered the greatest conspiracy against it that made it impossible to compre-hend. Jesus and His Father became more elusive. The Father that Jesus revealed to mankind disappeared from Jesus's Kingdom of God, only to be replaced by the God of Moses. Jesus knew that the Jews were setting up such platform, hence in His last trip to Jerusalem in the Temple, He said:

> *But woe unto you, scribes and Pharisees, hypocrites! For ye shut up the kingdom of heaven against men: for ye neither go in yourselves, neither suffer ye them that are entering to go in.*

> --- Matthew 23:13

Jesus also revealed this conspiracy in the parable of the tares (weeds).

> *The kingdom of heaven is likened unto a man who sowed good seed in his field: But while men slept, his enemy came and sowed tares among the wheat, and went his way. But when the blade was sprung up, and brought forth fruit, then appeared the tares also. So the servants of the householder came and said unto him, Sir, didst not thou sow good seed in thy field? From whence then hath it tares? He said unto them, an enemy hath done this. The servants said unto him, Wilt thou then that we go and gather them up? But he said, nay; lest while ye gather up the tares, ye root up also the wheat with them. Let both grow together until the harvest: and in the time of harvest I will say to the reapers, Gather ye together first the tares, and bind them in bundles to burn them: but gather the wheat into my barn.*

---Matthew 13: 24-30

The good seed is His Spirit, and the field is the human soul. The enemy is not the Devil. The 'enemies' are those who mixed the new wine with the old wine and patched the old clothes with the new clothes: the Jewish authorities and offered it to all who believe in Christ. They are those who integrated the Old Testament texts with the words of Jesus Christ. They are those who worked to destroy the works of Christ and called Him a deceiver of the people. In the end, they accused Him of blasphemy and condemned Him to death. That enemy persecuted His ordained apostles from one city to another and killed many of them, including Paul and early Disciples of Christ for the public proclamation of the secrets of Jesus's Kingdom of God, revealed to them by Christ. The scripts on which they recorded them were also destroyed. The information that I have given so far on Jesus's Kingdom of God and the deeper mysteries that I would reveal in this entire treatise is not new. The apostles and Paul had that information and martyred to silence them. The foreordained earthly fate of His apostle's troubled Jesus. Except for the apostle John, they were counted as sheep for slaughter and killed without mercy for the dissemination of that knowledge as Jesus had predicted:

> *But before all these, they shall lay their hands on you, and persecute you, delivering you up to the synagogues, and into prisons, being brought before kings and rulers for my name's sake. And it shall turn to you for a testimony. Settle it therefore in your hearts, not to meditate before what ye shall answer: For I will give you a mouth and wisdom, which all your adversaries shall not be able to gainsay nor resist. And ye shall be betrayed both by parents, and brethren, and kinsfolk's, and friends; and some of you shall they cause to be put to death. And ye shall be hated of all men for my name's sake. But there shall not a hair of your head perish. In your patience possess ye your souls.*

---Luke 21: 12-19

But why was the conspiracy necessary? What did the Jewish authorities see in Jesus's Kingdom of God that made them tremble with fear? In a meeting of the Sanhedrin; the high Priest, Caiaphas said that: "If we let this Jesus of Nazareth alone, as He is, all will believe in Him. The Romans will come and take away both our place and our nation." The Romans had already taken their nation and not interested in taking their positions as priests. Jesus's core message at that time was His Kingdom of God. What Caiaphas' statement reflected is this: if we do nothing to what Jesus was proclaiming, it will destroy our religion and our God. Ever since John the Baptist preached repentance, the Jews mobilized forces to prevent the opening of the heart of the people to the influence of this Jesus's

Kingdom of God. Jesus knew what they were doing that prompted Him to say:

> *And from the days of John the Baptist until now the kingdom of heaven suffereth violence, and the violent take it by force.*

> ---Matthew 11:12

Why were the Jews against Jesus Kingdom of God? They Jewish authorities understood the core elements in Jesus's Kingdom of God and its objectives. They knew that Jesus had introduced a new God the He called His Father that is hidden behind that Kingdom of God as the Creator. They had analyzed all His words on the Kingdom of God that He proclaimed, viewed then with His works and came to the conclusion that Jesus was also portraying Himself not only as a mediator of the Kingdom but also as a God. They knew that their God and Moses were not in it at all; and that the Kingdom was not the apocalyptic Messianic Kingdom they were expecting.

The conspiracy mounted against Jesus by the Jewish authorities was a multi-level disruptive and destructive activity that started with the proclamation of Jesus's kingdom of God and is still going on even as of today. The reason is simple: Jesus Kingdom of God is a threat to Judaism and the God they worship. When all the mysteries of Jesus's Kingdom of God are revealed-you have to read the entire book to grasp them-what you will find is the forgotten Spiritual bond in the mysteries that binds together all human spirits with the Spirit of His Father and not with the Spirit of the God of Moses and reveals Jesus as a Creator. The first thing the Jewish authorities did was to encourage people not to listen to Jesus's message of the Kingdom. Those people even called Jesus a deceiver of the people. That plot did not work, so they did the impossible. They conspired to condemn Jesus to death as to silence Him. Jesus was not condemned to death for the healing miracles or by claiming that He could forgive sins. For three years, Jesus preached that Kingdom of God that is rooted in His Father and not in the God that Moses revealed to them. He must be stopped.

Ever since the proclamation message of the impending Kingdom of God, many Christian communities, like the Psalmist and the Prophets, focused all their attention on the doxologies, and the glorious splendor of the Kingdom of God. The Kingdom is envisioned as a royal destiny where humans will receive the holy crown of glory. And the scripture is not lacking for such a support.

And when the Shepherd shall appear you shall receive a crown of glory that fades not away.

---Peter 5: 4

But what the scripture did not tell you is that he (Peter) who made the above statement had already received the Spirit of Christ and was working hard at that time, teaching humanity how to acquire the Spirit of Christ as to manifest its power and glory. The bearer of the message of the Kingdom of God died, He suffered violence. Jesus of Nazareth was crucified. He died for this Gospel of the Kingdom of God that mankind can benefit from it.

The subject on this current epiphany is on the great conspiracy mounted by the Jewish people as an obstacle to Jesus' Kingdom of God. Not all the Jews participated in this conspiracy. We were all deceived. The Christian leaders, scholars, you, and I became pawns on this conspiracy chessboard. As the Jewish religious leaders and the people they control listened to Jesus' message of the

Kingdom of God, they got disappointed and fearful. Fear is the greatest enemy of anything new. They took action. Inaction means the people of Israel would be deceived and would run after the new God—that Jesus called His Father—and His Kingdom. That would not be the first time the Jews turned away from their God to worship another God. It prompted Moses to break the first tablet of the Ten Commandments. Fear of loss of their positions as Jewish religious leaders drove them to initiate this conspiracy that deprived many from seeking insights that would enhance their knowledge of Christ and the Kingdom of God that He proclaims. I am committed to sharing what I recovered from the Gospel on Jesus' Kingdom of God and this great conspiracy against Him and the Kingdom of God that He introduced to the world. I did not get this information from any human being or from any book, but from the Gospel.

Despite all the weeds in the Gospel, what Jesus prescribed, proclaimed, and demonstrated are scattered in those records. The Jews thought they had eliminated features in the Gospel that would make it possible to understand it, but they are still there. Try it yourself. Take out one parable of Jesus' Kingdom of God. By the time you have gone through all of the other parables—if you understand their meaning—the message in the parable you removed will have been found in the other parables. Many have put words in Jesus' words and clothed Him with many things He did not say. He was even condemned to death and viciously killed as to silence Him, put an end to this new God and the proclamations of His Kingdom of God. It failed. Jesus' Kingdom of God took a quantum leap from Golgotha to a showcase display on Easter of what revealed the infinite power of His nature as a Creator and His Father as the true God and Lord of Creation.

It would seem that by hiding and disrupting this quantum leap that the great conspiracy succeeded, but it did not. What is the foundation of Jesus' Kingdom of God is still in the Gospel. I have presented it as I found it and will continue to do so to the end of the epistemology of the entire treatise. For now, it is very important to know the platform the Jews used in this great conspiracy. That would help us in finding the solution to the obstacle and liberate the new Christianity of Christ—to be free, like the wind.

How the Jews did it
The Jews were educated people and have excellent knowledge both in Jewish religion and in Christianity. The Jewish leaders fall into such a category. They knew what Jesus' Kingdom of God would do to their religion. The apostles were not that educated. They were not aware of the conspiracy. After the ascension of Jesus, they had continued to proclaim what their Master revealed to them on His Kingdom of God. The records on the mysteries of the mysteries of the Kingdom of God revealed to them by Christ vanished. Some that got to the Gospel were modified. Then the Jewish authorities resorted to killing the apostles as they proclaimed publicly the information on Jesus' Kingdom of God. The apostles were not killed because they were preaching that Jesus resurrected. In fact, the Pharisees believed in resurrection. So why, then, were they be killing the apostles?

It is important to note here that in the Gospel presented to us by the Jewish writers, the resurrection of Christ was portrayed as the center-point of all Jesus' activities. We were misled by the wrong information that the apostles were persecuted and killed for preaching about Jesus' resurrection. The truth is this: they were killed for the public revelation of the center point of all of Jesus' activities. They revealed the mysteries of Jesus' Kingdom of God. This persecution and modification of Gospel records, including the records of Paul's letters, continued throughout the crucible period of Christianity. All roads for the understanding of Jesus' Kingdom of God became impossible frontiers.

The Jewish leaders and scholars, slowly but surely chipped away at the foundation stone of Jesus Kingdom of God, eliminated what they deemed as great threats to their religious leadership positions, and rearranged its messages. They set to work, reconstructing and connecting Jesus' work with the Jewish religious system in order to replace the Father of Jesus with the God of Moses. What they did was to redirect the trajectory of Jesus' Kingdom of God from the Father and all mankind to *their* God and to the people of Israel and projected it to the apocalyptic Messianic Kingdom as envisioned by their prophets. Some of these apocalyptic prophecies were incorporated into the Gospel and put on the lips of Jesus Christ. What was recorded as Jesus's utterances on the Last Days in the Gospels of Mark 13:1-23, Matthew 42: 1-28, Luke 21: 5-24, all came from Old Testament references from Daniel 9:26, 27; Daniel 11:31 and Joel 2:2. Again what was recorded as Jesus's sayings on His second coming as recorded in the Gospels of Mark 13:24-27; Luke 21:25-28; Matthew 24:29-31, all came from Old Testament references of Isaiah 13:6-10, Ezekiel 32:7 and Daniel 7:13-14. The concepts of apocalyptic Son of Man, the Jewish prophetic Last Days, and Jesus as the expected Messiah that would come again are not featured in Jesus's Kingdom of God. Jesus is a universal Spirit. He is also here in this planet visible to those "who can hear with their eyes and hear with their ears," (Mark 8:18)

The biggest mistake in looking for the meaning of Jesus's Kingdom of God is to turn to the Old Testament literature. What is found in that literature is a Kingdom where the Jewish God rules as the Lord; a Kingdom where some can enter and others excluded. Moving forward along that trajectory, its future points to the apocalyptic Kingdom as envisioned by the Jewish Prophets-Ezekiel, Daniel and others. The Kingdom that Jesus proclaimed in parables and as He demonstrated, not just by the epitome of His life but also by the greatest of all His miracles: His death and resurrection, was a new entity. Nobody is excluded in that Kingdom. All-the Jews and the Gentiles-are invited to enter into that Kingdom. Jesus's Kingdom of God has nothing to do with an apocalyptic

Kingdom. It is a Kingdom that existed in this world, without anyone knowing of it, before Jesus came to this world, but it is not heaven or a spiritual realm where His Father reigns. Jesus learned from His Father how to use the power of that Kingdom in doing the same works as the Father.

However, the starting point for the ultimate understanding and interpretations of Jesus's kingdom of God and its mysteries is to find out what Jesus did with our only gift from His Father. This gift is the Father's love, mercy, righteousness, compassion, forgiveness, or protection from evil. All these are inside the gift box but are not the core element of that gift. The gift of the Father is His Spirit given to us through Jesus Christ. The knowledge of what Jesus did for us with that gift opens all the closed doors of Jesus's Kingdom of God and its mysteries. Deeper revelations of Jesus Kingdom of God and its mysteries are the subjects that I explored in subsequent epiphanies of this treatise.

We cannot know what Jesus's Kingdom of God is for us today without knowing what it is. The misconceptions of Jesus's Kingdom of God cast a dark shadow in the revelation of the task from His Father that Jesus completed for us. It misdirected Jesus's new Christianity to a dark alley. It plays a profound influence in our lives, as many are forced to seek earthly treasures and political powers. It created corrupt Churches that are devoid on what the new Christianity of Christ, prescribed, proclaimed and demonstrated. With no knowledge of this truth, Christianity ended in a blind faith and hope. The universal message and freedom offered by Jesus's Kingdom of God was locked up in the closet.

Jesus Christ is not a prophet who usually started his proclamations with "Thus saith the Lord." Jesus started many of His proclamations with "I say unto you," like a Lord. If Jesus promoted and gave more revelations of the God of Israel and projected the Kingdom as a Kingdom of Israel where their God reigns, why would they have condemned Him to death and subsequently persecuted and killed the apostles?

The Jews had combined the new wine and the old wine and offered it to the Christians. Many of the Christians that drank it never tasted the new wine as it was never truly offered to them. The Jews won! The New Testament became—as they hoped—the Jewish liberation. The Old Testament became the canonized Christian Holy Book. The God of Moses was enthroned as the Father of Jesus who reigned and created all things. The meaning of Jesus' Kingdom of God was secretly locked up. The apostolic documents that revealed the mysteries of Jesus' Kingdom of God as was revealed to them by their Master were destroyed. Jesus and eleven of the apostles and Paul and some early Christians were permanently silenced. There was no escape for the Christians and their leaders.

This great conspiracy platform crafted and executed by the Jews is real and still going on today as shown by the following facts, that any introduction of Jesus' Kingdom of God in literature starts with the Kingdom of Yahweh in the Old Testament and ends with Jesus' Kingdom of God viewed with the Jewish lens. Religious dictionaries and many literatures from scholars started with such definitions.

In the teaching of Jesus, "Kingdom of God" is a phrase denoting his adherence to the expectation of salvation developed from the Israel's belief in God as the King of the people.

---The New Schaff-Herzog Encyclopedia of Religious Knowledge, Volume VI, p334

The Kingdom of God lay at the heart of Jesus' teaching. As proclaimed by Jesus, the kingdom of God had continuity with OT promise as well as with the Jewish apocalyptic thinking, but differed from them in important respects. For example it denoted God's eternal rule rather than an earthly Kingdom, its scope was universal rather than limited to the Jewish nation, and it was imminent and potentially present in him rather than a vague future hope being inextricably connected with his own person and mission.

---Dictionary of the Gospel of Jesus and the Gospel.
Editors: Joel B. Green et al, p. 417

The Kingdom of God is God's universal dominion over all things, thereby he preserves, protects, gives, laws to, and regulates all he creates and can dispense favors or judgment as he pleases.

---1 Chronicles 29:11; Psalm CXLV: 12. Excerpt on the Kingdom of God from the Popular and Critical Bible Encyclopedia and Scriptural Dictionary, Volume 2, p. 1024-25

The saint's new-covenant state and the work of saving grace in their heart are called the 'kingdom' of God and the 'kingdom' of heaven. Therein God erects his throne in their heart, gives laws and privileges to their souls, render them heavenly minded and meet to enter the heavenly glory.

---Matthew 6:33; 8:31; Luke 17:20-21 Excerpt on the Kingdom of God from the Popular and Critical Bible Encyclopedia and Scriptural Dictionary, Volume 2, p. 1024-25

Jesus' message of the Kingdom of God runs through all the forms and statements of the prophecy which, taking its color from the Old Testament, announces the day of judgment and the visible government of God in the future, up to the idea of an inward coming of the kingdom, starting with Jesus' message and the beginning...The kingdom of God is the rule of God; but of God in the hearts of individuals, it is God himself in his power.

---Adolf von Harnack on What is Christianity, p 52, 56

The Hebrew-Christian faith expresses its hope in terms of the Kingdom of God. The Biblical idea of the kingdom is rooted deeply in the Old Testament and is grounded in the confidence that there is one eternal living God who has revealed Himself to men and who has a purpose for the human race which He has chosen to accomplish through Israel.

---George Ladd, the Gospel of the Kingdom, p. 14

The Jews piped the distorted message about Jesus' Kingdom of God so loudly that the Churches and Christian scholars danced to that tune. We see evidence of this dance in the various interpretations of that kingdom. All their definitions of Jesus' Kingdom of God point to the Old Testament. As a result, it lost its meaning, and Jesus' Kingdom of God, designed for all mankind with the spirit of His Father, became the kingdom of the God of Abraham, Moses, and the prophets for the people of Israel. It was subsequently modified to accept few people outside Judaism. Some of the Jewish writers of the Gospel contributed immensely to this conspiracy.

What happened to Paul is not only despicable but horrifying. Paul was imprisoned in chains for two years in Rome. At last, the Roman judge found no fault in Paul and released him. During that trial, Paul must have mounted such a defense that his trial before other Roman appointed governors would be considered child's play. But where is the record of that trial? Who destroyed it? For what the Jews considered the last insult on the Law and for the public proclamations of all his revelations of that Jesus and His Kingdom of God, Paul was beheaded after he was released from the Roman prison.

I have left this page BLANK in memory of the apostles, Paul and others who were murdered for proclaiming the revelations of Jesus' Kingdom of God.

The Scribes and the Pharisees who developed the blue print for this conspiracy knew that:

1. To enter into it is to abandon their God and embrace the Father, the new God that Jesus proclaimed. They did not see their God inside Jesus' Kingdom of God.
2. To embrace Jesus' Kingdom of God is to believe in Jesus Christ, and that in essence is also to believe in the Father that sent Him to this world. They knew about their God that revealed Himself to Moses and spoke to Abraham and the prophets, but no one had seen this new Father of Jesus. They had, on many occasions, asked Jesus to tell them who this Father is. Jesus, again and again, refused to do so. To believe in Jesus' Kingdom of God would destroy their religion, as all the people would follow Jesus and abandon Judaism.
3. To support Jesus' concept of His Kingdom is to support all the things He said about Himself on this Kingdom as true

In essence, it is to force them to acknowledge Jesus' divine authority. The Jewish leaders knew that without this knowledge, people would not understand many of His words and His mission. So they took action, and they succeeded. For more than two thousand years, nobody—from the end of the crucible period of Christianity to the present time—understood the meaning of Jesus' Kingdom of God. In all of the expositions, the Church and the Christian theologians always start with the statement: It is the core message of Jesus, but Jesus did not reveal its meaning. However, what everyone—the Jews, the Church, the Christians, and the Scholars—did not know is that Jesus Christ left markers that can *never* be erased in His Gospel, markers that reveal all He wanted us to know about His Kingdom of God and its mysteries. Jesus said that: "There is nothing hidden that cannot be revealed."

Jesus revealed the meaning of His Kingdom of God, not just in words, but with demonstration. Jesus demonstrated it by:

The exhibition of its power.
The epitome of His life
Display of greatest miracle of all time: the recreation of Himself by His death and resurrection—an infallible evidence that cannot be erased.
The gift of His glorified risen Spirit to the apostles on the day of Pentecost

It is for this reason that Jesus' Kingdom of God survived the gruesome conspiracy and it is still a force—although forgotten—that still lives, striving in its trajectory to achieve its objectives and goals. The fact that I am able to uncover this conspiracy against Jesus' Kingdom of God gives me hope and confidence in Jesus Christ and in the divine origin of that kingdom from His Father. It triumphed as prescribed, proclaimed by Jesus, and will continue to do so, as it powers all things—regardless of conspiracies and opposites—to achieves its goals: the divine trinity of the human souls with the Father and Himself and the revelation of Jesus and His Father to the world.

Jesus' Kingdom of God is the life-line of all His works and words that give mankind insight to who He is, the nature of His Father, and what human life is. It allowed us to have a glimpse into the spiritual world s of His Father. It empowers us to work purposely that we can also, like His apostles, see His glory. Today, to most people, Jesus' Kingdom of God is a vague or empty entity. They do not see themselves in it. I believe that I have recovered the meaning of Jesus' Kingdom of God from the Gospel and un-covered the great conspiracy mounted against it. You will not fully comprehend the Father that Jesus introduced to the world, who Jesus is, who we are, and our destiny without true knowledge of Jesus' Kingdom of God and its mysteries.

The misconceptions of Jesus's Kingdom of God cast a dark shadow in the revelation of the task from His Father that Jesus completed for us. It formed a stumbling block on all attempts to know why Jesus died. It misdirected Jesus's new Christianity to a dark alley. It plays a profound influence in our lives, as many are forced to seek earthly treasures and political powers. It created corrupt Churches that are devoid on what the new Christianity of Christ, prescribed, proclaimed and demonstrated. With no knowl-edge of this truth, Christianity ended in a blind faith and hope. The universal message and freedom offered by Jesus's Kingdom of God was locked up in the closet.

It is not my intention in this epiphany to give an overview on the works of scholars or even the Church in regards to Jesus' king-dom of God. There are just too many different interpretations, even among and within the church groups. Neither do I pro-pose to offer a comparison of what I recovered from the Gospel with their definition on these subjects. My aim, rather, is to draw worldwide attention to the conspiracy that I have uncovered and redirect people to the trajectory of that Kingdom that leads to

God, the Father of Jesus and give that vital information to all the people of the world that we are potential members of that kingdom, It is for this reason that we must seek world peace, love, and care for one another. We have all the potentials to activate Jesus's Kingdom of God within us and manifest that experience to the world. It is my hope that with what I have uncovered, mankind will be able to remove the "beam from our eyes" that has blinded us for nearly two thousand years and see clearly the road to the wedding feast, that we may go and drink the new wine and have experience of Jesus' new Christianity. This is our ascension to the path of our glory.

CHAPTER 12

THE MYSTERIES OF JESUS'S KINGDOM OF GOD

And He (Jesus) turned him unto his disciples, and said privately, Blessed are the eyes which see the things that ye see: For I tell you, that many prophets and kings have desired to see those things which ye see, and have not seen them; and to hear those things which ye hear, and have not heard them.

—Luke 10:23-24

A diligent exploration of the words and the works of Christ as recorded in the Gospel, gives an insight into the mysteries of Jesus Kingdom of God. First, you have to know the meaning of Jesus's Kingdom of God, as to be able to have a glimpse into its mysteries. To gain insight into its mysteries, we have to look at all Jesus's words and works with the lens of His Kingdom of God and follow Jesus all the way to Golgotha, to the day of His resurrection, to Bethany from where He ascended to heaven and review the manifestations of the promised gift of His Father that came on the day of the Pentecost. It was for this reason that Jesus did not reveal verbally the mysteries of the Kingdom He proclaimed. To have a glimpse into all the mysteries of His Kingdom of God, you have to follow Him all the way, observe and be with the apostles in Jerusalem on the day of the Pentecost. I have in this series given a preparatory platform to stand on in the exploration of deeper meaning of Jesus's Kingdom of God and its mysteries.

Jesus's Kingdom of God is a profound metaphysical facade that allowed humankind to glimpse into previously unrevealed history of the mysteries of God, the Father that Jesus revealed as a living true God and the Lord of Creation. It empowered Jesus's everlasting miracle of the earthly stages of human creation that revealed His role in human creation. That miracle of life, demonstrated by Jesus through His death and resurrection, opened the portals of the spiritual world of Christ and for the first time in its history, humankind had a glimpse into what Jesus Christ and His Father had been doing all along: creating spiritual beings. By following what happened on the fiftieth day after the ascension of Jesus Christ, the divine origin of all His words and works were validated by the fulfillment of that gift that came on the day of Pentecost. It was an event that not only confirmed the infinite creative power of Jesus's Kingdom of God, but an act that changed the mysteries of His Kingdom of God from *mysterium tremendum* (fearful mystery) to *mysterium fascinans* (fascinating mystery). The mysteries of Jesus's Kingdom of God-the pillar and the foundation of the truth of His words and works-holds all the mysteries of the Christian Faith. They are rooted in what was finished at Golgotha. The mysteries of Jesus's Kingdom of God were revealed to the apostles and Paul.

For this cause I Paul, the prisoner of Jesus Christ for you Gentiles, If ye have heard of the dispensation of the grace of God which is given me to you-ward: How that by revelation he made known unto me the mystery; (as I wrote afore in few words, Whereby, when ye read, ye may understand my knowledge in the mystery of Christ) Which in other ages was not made known unto the sons of men, as it is now revealed unto his holy apostles and prophets by the Spirit.

---Ephesians 3: 1-5

Jesus's Kingdom of God is a propulsive divine power propelling human life to its eternity, revealing in its trajectory, the mysteries of who Jesus is, the nature of His Father, who we are, why we are here, the intrinsic value of human life and our destiny. All these revelations, dominated by Jesus's Kingdom of God, as proclaimed, prescribed and demonstrated by Christ in His words and works, are the mysteries of His Kingdom that were hidden from wise men and the Jewish prophets before Jesus came to this world. The connecting link to all the mysteries of Jesus's Kingdom of God is the cross.

This current epiphany on Jesus's kingdom of God and its mysteries is a prolog to establish you for more facts on what I decoded from the works and words of Christ, according to the revelations of the mysteries of the Kingdom of God hidden from us since after the crucible period of Christianity. It is my hope that in the end, you may be able to comprehend 'what is the breath, and the length, and the depth, and the height' of all the mysteries of Jesus's Kingdom of God that unraveled in His everlasting miracle of the earthly stages of human creation, and to know the love of Christ and respond to His call to enter into His Kingdom and have it within you.

End

BIBLIOGRAPHY

Beasley Murray. *Jesus and the Kingdom of God*. The Paternoster Press. UK 1986

Bornkamm, Günther. *Jesus of Nazareth*. Trans. Irene McLuskey and Fraser McLuskey. Minneapolis: Fortress P, 1995.

Borsch Fredrick. *God's Parable*. The Westminister Press Philadelphia. USA 1975

Bright John. *The Kingdom of God*. Abingdon Press. USA 1953

Burton, Trochmorton Jr. *Gospel Parallels*. Nashville: Thomas Nelson Publishers, 1979.

Candlish James. *The Kingdom of God Biblically and Historically considered*. HardPress Publishers. Miami, Fl. USA. 1882

Dodd C. H. *The Parables of the Kingdom*. Charles Scribner;s & Sons. USA

Donahue John. *The Gospel in Parables*. Fortress Press. USA 1990

Dych William. *Thy Kingdom come*. Herder and Herder Books. USA 1999

Enumah, Festus. MD. *The Innocent Blood and Judas Iscariot*. Guardian Books: Canada, 2002.

Enumah Festus MD. *The Father's Business and the Spiritual Cross*. Published in Charleston.USA 2014

Fallows, Samuel Rt. Rev. *Bible Encyclopedia and Scriptural Dictionary*. Chicago: The Howard-Severance Company, 1907.

Fite Warner. *Jesus the Man*. Harvard University Press. USA. 1946

Fosdick Harry. *The Man from Nazareth*. Harper and Brothers. NY. USA 1949

Fuellenbach John. *The Kingdom of God*. Orbis Books. NY. 1995

Häring, Bernard. *The Law of Christ*. Trans. Edwin G. Kaiser. Westminster: The Newman P, 1963.

Harnack, Adolf. *What is Christianity?* New York: Harper & Brothers Publishers, 1957.

Holland Henry Scott. *God's City and the coming of the Kingdom*. Longmans, Green & Co
NY. USA 1987

The Holy Bible, Original King James Version. Gordonsville: Dugan Publishers Inc., 1985.

Jackson Samuel Macauley. *The new Schaff-Herzog Encyclopedia of Religious Knowledge*.

Baker Book House. Grand Rapid. Michigan. USA 1950

Jeremias, Joachim..*The Parables of Jesus*. Prentice-Hall. USA 1963

Kaufmann Walter (Introducer) *Religion from Tolstoy to Camus*. Harper Torch Books. N.Y. 1961

Kittay, Eva F. *Metaphor*. Oxford: Clarendon P, 1989

Ladd George. *The Gospel of the Kingdom*. William B. Eerdmans Publishers. USA

Lakoff, George, and Mark Johnson. *Metaphors We Live By*. Chicago: University of Chicago P, 1980.

Linwood Urban *A short history of Christian thoughts*. Oxford University Press 1995.

Mclnerny, D. Q. *Being Logical*. New York: Random House, 2004.

Pelikan, Jaroslav. *Jesus Through the Centuries*. New York: Harper & Row, 1985.

Pink Arthur. *The Beatitudes and the Lord's Prayer*. Baker Books. USA 1979

Richards, Lawrence O. *The Word Bible Handbook*. Waco: Word, Inc., 1982.

Sanday, William. *The International Critical Commentary on the Holy Scripture of the Old and New Testaments.* New York: Charles Scribners Sons, 1920.

Schillebeeckx, Edward. *Jesus: An experiment in Christology.* New York: Seabury, 1979.

Sheen, Fulton J. *Life of Christ.* New York: Image Books Doubleday. 1958.

Schweitzer Albert *The mystery of the Kingdom of God.* Dodd, Mead Publishers. USA 1914

Simkhovitch, Vladimir. *Toward the Understanding of Jesus.* New York: The MacMillan Company,1925.

Thompson Marianne Meye. *The Promise of the Father.* Westminister John Knox Press. USA. 2000

Tolstoy Leo. *The Kingdom of God is within you.* University of Nebraska Press USA. 1984

Townshend, George. *The Heart of the Gospel.* London: Templar Printing Works, 1939.

Wesley John. *The nature of the Kingdom.* Bethany House Publishers. USA. 1979.

Wood, et al. *Immanuel Kant: Religion within the Boundaries of Mere Reason And Other Writings.* Cambridge: Cambridge UP, 1998

Dr. Festus Enumah has arranged for part of his share of the proceeds from all his books to be donated to Samuel A. Enumah Africancer Foundation, www.africancer.org, a public, charitable nonprofit 501(c) (3) corporation registered in the state of Georgia, USA. The objective of the foundation is to help develop and build the infrastructure in sub-Saharan Africa for cancer control services, focusing on cancer education, prevention, early detection and treatment. The aim of the foundation is to help reduce the deaths from cancer and improve cancer patients' quality of life.

ABOUT THE AUTHOR

Dr. Festus Enumah was born in Nigeria, on January 21, 1943. He graduated from the University of Ibadan Medical School in Nigeria, and completed his internship and residency in general surgery at Cook County Hospital, Chicago, Illinois. He subsequently went to M. D. Anderson Cancer Center in Houston, Texas, where he successfully completed a fellowship in thoracic surgical oncology. He is board certified by the American Board of Surgery and the Royal College of Physicians and Surgeons of Canada.

He is married to Lois Bronersky-Enumah, who is also a board certified family physician. They live in Columbus, Georgia and have four children. Dr. Enumah is the Founder and the President of Samuel A. Enumah Africancer Foundation. His first book, *The Innocent Blood and Judas Iscariot,* was published in 2002. His second book, *The Father's Business and the Spiritual Cross,* was published in 2014.